LOSS OF CENTER, LOSS OF SOUL

The Plight of the
Global Spiritual Community

In loving memory of Almeda (my mother), and our shared experiences in the days of our joy, in the times of our pains, and all that is enduring she blessed me with; and, Donald, (my father), for whom there is an empty space only he can fill. And, in recognition of the long line of my strong and beautiful African ancestors, and those of us, still today, navigating life in a strange and alien place.

LOSS OF CENTER, LOSS OF SOUL

The Plight of the
Global Spiritual Community

Written By
Rev. Rodney Eugene Alexander, M.Div., Ph.D.

Front Cover Design By
Jesse Burrell
of **Top Level Designs by Jesse**

Back Cover Design
Sun Child Wind Spirit

Proofread By
Mylia Tiye Mal Jaza

LOSS OF CENTER, LOSS OF SOUL:
The Plight of the Global Spiritual Community
Copyright © 2017, Rodney Eugene Alexander
All Rights Reserved.

ISBN-10: 1543196314   ISBN-13: 978-1543196313

Author Contact
Rev. Rodney Alexander, M.Div., Ph.D.
realexander1002@gmail.com
www.TransformTranscend.org

Self-Publishing Associate
BePublished.Org - Chicago
Dr. Mary M. Jefferson
(972) 880-8316
www.bepublished.org
mari@bepublished.org

Imprint of Record
CreateSpace On-Demand Publishing
7290-B Investment Drive
Charleston, SC 29418
4900 LaCross Road
North Charleston, SC 29406

First Edition. Series Volume One.
Printed In the USA.
Recycled Paper Encouraged.

- TABLE OF CONTENT -

Preface 9

A Childhood Reflection 11

Introduction 15

Bibliography 179

Index 185

Chapter	Title	Page
1	The Global Spiritual Community: Universality, Multiplicity and Significance	17
2	Founders of Religion: The Relational Center	29
3	This Thing Called Life: The Sum of Our Relationships	40
4	Life: The Gold Standard of Spiritual Experience	47
5	Spiritual Life, Spirituality, and Religion: First Things	54

6   Relational Spirituality (R/S): The   91
    Relational Priority

7   Relational Spirituality (R/S): The   117
    Indispensable Relational Qualities

8   Relational Spirituality (R/S): The   134
    4 T's: Transition, Transformation,
    Transcendence, and Triumph

9   The 4T's: What They Look Like in   139
    an Actual Life

10 Relational Spirituality (R/S): A   175
    Reflective Summation

PREFACE

C.G. Jung said, "What happens to a man is characteristic of him." This is a profound psycho-spiritual insight, which, in today's world, he would most certainly have us take in a gender inclusive sense.

I understand him to mean that the essential direction, development, and outcome of an individual's life turn principally upon the dispositional qualities inherent in his/her personality and character. Experience, observation, and knowledge, over a lifetime, confirm that this is true. Yet, it is an *incomplete truth*.

What must be included here, and what we must also understand, is that an individual's personality and character do not appear in a vacuum. They are revealed and exhibited in a constellation of relationships. What happens to her/him, what is characteristic of him/her, and how life turns out for her/him, unfolds (in its fullness), is inextricably linked to the *realm of relationship* – the subject of this book. My purpose is to "bring to light" the experience, thought, significance, and language of Relational Spirituality (R/S) for the Global Spiritual

Community (GSC). My hope is that, once again, this community (as a collective), might return to its true *Center: The Centrality of Relationship in spiritual life, spirituality, and religion.*

Everything of significance that I have ever experienced and everything that has happened to me (past and present) has, and continues to occur within a multifaceted constellation of relationships. Things that have not happened to me and experiences that I have not had are due to the absence of certain relationships in which they might have occurred.

Most folks have, and know, at least one of their parents; many have, and know, both. In a very real sense, I've had to find my way in life without either.

There's my relationship with my mother, whom I love. The wound goes deep, the hurt is real, and the pain substantial. A *reflection* I wrote, describing a significant, unforgettable moment we shared together, expresses my feelings (then and now) about our relationship.

A CHILDHOOD REFLECTION

Ever think back to childhood days? Ever been in a setting where you were asked to recall, reflect upon, and share one of the happiest moments you ever experienced as a child? What did you come up with? Were there many, few, or sadly, none? Are there recollections of happy moments, memories of which will last a lifetime? Or was it disturbing, troublesome and difficult, because truly happy moments as a young child were hard to remember as such moments were rare, almost non-existent? Whatever the case may be, childhood memories have to do with relationships with Mom and/or Dad, brothers and/or sisters, extended family, friends, and the larger community. Today, my thoughts go to my mother. The happiest moment of my childhood, that I remember in relation to my mother, occurred when I was an impressionable preschooler.

It was sunny, warm and bright, a beautiful day in spring. My mom had downtown shopping to do, and took me along. I don't know why she took only me, (two brothers and a sister were at home). Whatever the reason, it was mom and me, I was with my mother, we were together, I liked it and it was very special to me. Downtown was, as usual, bustling and busy. As we walk up, down, and across busy streets, going in and out of stores and peering into window displays, my mother held my hand. I felt so good inside, as we walked hand and hand together. I remember, as she spoke to me, receiving her full attention, as she shared with me some motherly guidance and insights fit for a preschooler, as we went along our way. When she looked at me, it was direct; she gave me her full gaze! My heart blazed with joy! I was experiencing a deep relational bond and connection.

I was experiencing her love and specific interest in me. On that day, during that downtown shopping trip, my mother, through her actions and words demonstrated her intimate interest and care for me! And I felt affirmed, valued and accepted by the single most important individual in my life at that time, my mother.

Why did, and does, this experience with my mother stand out as one of the happiest of memories in my childhood? Because it was the first time in my earliest conscious memory, that my mother related to me in a way that I knew she loved me. That incredible feeling of belonging and connection never happened again. It was to be the last time.

Mom's affirmation, affection, acceptance and care that shined so brightly on that day never occurred again. I am now older than my mother was back then. What happened?

No matter how I try to understand my mother and our relationship, the wound and hurt around this memory, that I carry about, though underground and unconscious, is not dormant as one might suppose, but actively alive, surfacing when it will. And for a time, I'm in pain once again, over the loss.

But there is a powerfully dynamic spiritual truth that I know experientially. It transforms fragmentation into wholeness. It is an antidote that comforts and heals. And so, to others like me, who know from experience, what I've shared, I recommend and counsel the following simple, yet profound affirmation:

"THOUGH MY MOTHER AND FATHER FORSAKE ME, THE LORD RECEIVES ME."
(Psalm 27:10)

Thank you God, thank you God,
thank you God!

Then, there's my father, whom I also love, who for example, was absent from much of my life (this does not mean that he was a scoundrel). I have come to know and understand his situation, and the prevailing circumstances. But how I've wished throughout life, that I had someone I knew and called dad. The absence/loss of these two fundamental relationships posed many challenges and not a few obstacles that I have had to unflinchingly face and progressively conquer (in gratitude to God and a constellation of supportive *relationships*). Yes, our relationships can and do harm and hurt us. Yet, they are also, as these pages attest to, the very instruments that are essential to/for our psycho-spiritual, and emotional health, healing, and well-being.

INTRODUCTION

Spiritual life, spirituality, and religion are primary and ultimate matters for me. I am compelled to express, explore, and expound, as a minister, leader, educator, counselor, guide, companion on the spiritual journey, what I feel, believe, and know, to be the essence of spiritual experience.

This requires wisdom, humility, experience, knowledge, and the ability to discern, distinguish, and clarify (out of a multiplicity of spiritual interests, considerations, and concerns), what, after all, actually matters most in spiritual experience.

This is a perennial subject for inquiry and exploration. I believe such a task calls for, and insists upon, an unambiguous and unequivocal response. If there is no clarity here, spiritual experience sours, spiritual leadership fails, and criticism of spiritual claims is justified. Our inquiry asks, where is the emphasis on *relationships* (their quality or lack thereof)? Where is the intentional engagement to improve, enrich and enhance relationships within, between and among all communities of faith, belief and practice? Who should do this, and how? Where is the relational concern? Where is the centrality of relationships?

I focus (as many in the global spiritual community do not), on **actual relationships**. While many things in spiritual experience matter, I contend that relationships (their quality or lack thereof) matter most, more than any other competing interests, considerations, and concerns. In these pages, I constructively, but tenaciously, set forth my perspective, which places **the relational experience at the center of spiritual life**. I persuade all who are vested in relationships (all types and kinds) to do the same.

Rodney Eugene Alexander (Oluwafemi)
April 2017

CHAPTER ONE
The Global Spiritual Community: Universality, Multiplicity, and Significance

"In understanding an inquiry, we must first from the beginning possess a minimum of knowledge of the meaning of that about which we are trying to inquire. No inquiry starts out of nothing. In asking the first question, we must anticipate something of the nature of that which we ask about, because otherwise we would not know in what direction to proceed or whether the result of our inquiry will be an answer to the question."

Rabbi Abraham Joshua Heschel

Taking Heschel's counsel to heart, the ***Global Spiritual Community (GSC)*** consists of individuals and groups within all the world's religions (large and small, well known, least known), faiths, traditions, spiritual paths, and related movements from earliest times to the present. As such, it is a ***universal phenomenon*** (multi-cultural, multi-ethnic, multi-lingual, multi-national and multi-tribal). It is, in fact, a living mosaic of all that is human.

As universal, spirituality/religion is experienced and expressed in and through diverse human particularities of culture, thought, language, speech, ethnicity, tribe and temperament etc. Far from being a mystery, spiritual life, spirituality, and religion are common, usual, and ordinary realities that reveal the full range of human experience, behavior, and endeavor. Given this universality, spiritual experience is not the domain of a single group, individual, culture or class.

Experiencing, exploring, defining, understanding, articulating, explaining, interpreting, and the teaching of religion are not the exclusive prerogatives of any one group or individual. Spiritual experience is comprehended best, and more fully understood, appreciated, honored, and respected, when seen through many eyes, experiences, and places.

A credible inquiry into spiritual/religious phenomena, worthy of one's time, interests, and energy, will include multiple experiences, perspectives, and points of view. Though there is reluctance on the part of many, efforts must be made to move beyond the confines, limitations, and boundaries of one's own particular religion, without betraying the essentials of one's own particular beliefs.

It follows that our inquiry into the GSC, is both *comparative and inclusive.* The central aim/mission of the

GSC is rooted in what may be called its *Global Spiritual Enterprise (GSE)*: Engaging, directing, and leading the peoples of the world (individually and collectively) in, and through, constructive and beneficial, life altering spiritual experiences, expressions, and pursuits. In a time of globalization, we look at issues, events, and situations in terms of their global cultural, governmental, economic, and political significance and impact.

An inquiry into the GSC is no exception. We look for the "big religious picture" here. Our inquiry is not a focus on this, that, or the other religion, spiritual enterprise, or endeavor, but on *all*. As all are actors on a global scale in the issues, events, situations and problems of, with, and in relation to religion in the 21st century. In this approach, complexity does not overwhelm, the derailing powers of diversion, distraction, and deflection are eliminated; and confusion, exhaustion, futility and despair are held in check.

For all of its diversity, constituents of the GSC share common cause and concern for what are the *foundational pillars of spiritual experience*: *spiritual life* (which is inherently possessed by all and cannot be given or taken away), *spirituality* (the versions, varieties, and various ways spiritual life is experienced and expressed), and *religion* (the external expression of spiritual life in terms of systems, structures, forms, and institutions). In speaking of the GSC, these terms, as defined above, will be used throughout the book. Our inquiry is not insignificant. Anthropologist, Annemarie de Waal Malefijt (by way of historical overview), attests to the fact that religion has impacted virtually every aspect of human experience.

> Religion is one of the most important aspects of culture studied by anthropologists and other social scientists. Not only is it found in every known human society, it also interacts with other cultural institutions. It finds expression in material culture, in human behavior, and in value systems, morals and ethics. It interacts with systems of family organization, marriage, economics, law, and politics; it enters into the realm of medicine, science, and technology; and it has inspired rebellions and wars as well as sublime works of art. No other cultural institution presents so vast a range of expression and implication.

C.G. Jung (1875 - 1961) renowned psychologist and healer of the psyche, describes religion from a psychological perspective, in this way:

> Religions are psychotherapeutic systems in the truest sense of the word, and on the grandest scale...they are the avowal and recognition of the soul, and at the same time the revelation of the soul's nature...Everything it is and asserts, touches the human soul so closely that psychology least of all can afford to overlook it.

Both statements convincingly confirm that the **universality, multiplicity, and significance** of spiritual life, spirituality, and religion are transparent realities only the naïve can dismiss or deny.

As to its significance, the GSC, for better or worse, in weal and woe, is customarily viewed as, and expected to be a trustworthy, and reliable expositor, definer, demonstrator, and disseminator of all matters and things of spiritual experience. It basically functions (in its variant forms), as the global keeper, guardian, and custodian of spiritual leadership and guidance for those who look unto it for such direction.

Demographics show that most of the world's present population is religious. Less than a third is considered variously secular. As most of the world is religious, and religion is expected to be a beneficent blessing and light in the world, why (it must be asked) is the world adrift in seas of mayhem and darkness? What hopeful, helpful, and healing ameliorations to our global problems are to be found within, or from the GSC, when **religion** is itself a central component of those problems? Why is this entity, in the minds of many, odiously suspect? It's legitimacy, credibility, and authenticity, more than being called into question, is unapologetically dismissed and rejected by an increasing number within, and many outside of it?

Commenting on the "religious problem," Rabbi Abraham Heschel puts the matter this way:

> It is customary to blame secular science and anti-religious philosophy for the eclipse of religion in modern society. It would be more honest to blame religion for its defeats. Religion declined not because it was refuted, but because it became irrelevant, dull, oppressive, and insipid. When faith is completely replaced by creed, worship by discipline, love by habit; when

the crisis of today is ignored because of the splendor of the past; faith becomes an heirloom rather than a living fountain; when religion speaks in the name of authority rather than the voice of compassion, its message becomes meaningless

There are individuals and groups within the GSC doing commendable service, when, how, and where they can. They are the minority, the faithful few. But, we know, they do not carry the day, labor under great odds, and are regularly frustrated, often to the point of despair.

Our inquiry addresses the GSC as a collective. As a collective it has an immense foot-print in much of the seemingly intractable and exacting spiritual, religious, cultural, socio-economic, and political problems of our times. At times, its responses to the national and international crises of our times, its own moral and ethical beliefs can hardly be distinguished from many of its secular counterparts which make only a relative claim to such guiding values and principles in daily life and conduct around our contemporary world.

Action-less declarations, documents, conferences, symposiums, talk of peace, love, justice, and ecumenical prayers of the pious, are quickly followed by attitudes and behaviors that on various levels support, encourage, and embolden national, state, regional, political, tribal, ethnic, cultural, gender, and sexual violence, terror, and war. Always, of course, complete with *self-serving/self-seeking* religious rationalizations and all sorts of manufactured spiritual justifications.

Some, in the GSC, erroneously believe, contrary to all historical fact, that religious government and rule (theocracies) are morally, ethically, and spiritually superior to governments that are decidedly secular. This has never been demonstrated. The truth is that both forms of government, and the people who design them, inevitably find themselves inextricably entangled, enmeshed and bound to the abusive and addictive opiates of sovereign power, unquestioned authority, and absolute control over all aspects of life.

Under such circumstances does it really matter which government is at the helm? Both are suspect and both are complicit. The similarities are so great, we can call it a draw. There is no difference between religious corruption and secular corruption, corruption on the right and corruption on the left. Each forestalls, blocks, impedes, is inimical to, and threatens peace, justice, and a well-ordered society. In the midst of these forms of corruption one petitions Divine blessings, and the other, the aggrandizing divinities of secular wealth, greed, favorable winds and good fortune. As history demonstrates, the situation becomes even more dire when these entities unite and act in collusion. Neither can pretentiously claim one is morally and ethically superior to the other. Both are rightly suspect and culpable for incalculable damages to their respective societies and cultures. But we are specifically interested in the religiously inclined and spiritually engaged people throughout the world.

Don't Blink: The Human Factor

The GSC is a collective of human beings. This is a significant fact. Because it serves to temper our critique and assessment of it, it reminds us that spiritual life, spirituality and religion are incontestably real to billions of adherents and advocates representing a multiplicity of faiths, paths and traditions.

These diverse experiences and expressions can be simple, basic, complex and profound, masculine and feminine, transgendered, nationalistic, tribal, cultural, and political.

What this means (and many will disagree), is that, there are no **religions, faiths, or spiritual paths,** apart from the people who represent them. Religions are reflections of the people espousing them. If religions are perceived as selfishly self-serving, self-seeking, unjust, compassionless, duplicitous, deceitful, profiteering, abusive, and oppressive, or loving, kind, merciful, just, accepting, affirming, and empathetic, *it is because their adherents and followers are.* If we remember that *religions are the external expressions of spiritual life,* in terms of human systems, structures, organizations, and institutions, it becomes clear, (and we can conclude), that, **People are their religions** *and they act/react humanly before they do religiously. More often than not, human interests, wants, and desires trump those that are technically religious, theological, doctrinal or creedal.*

As such, the people of the world who are religiously inclined and spiritually engaged, can and will, (as situations dictate), be evocative, temperamental, joyful, accepting, affirming, encouraging, peaceful, emotive, intellectual, ignorant, fraudulent, misleading, harsh, cognitive, sexual, erotic, mystical, mysterious, inexplicable, deplorable, depressing, delusional, destructive, judgmental, immoral, violent, and murderous. They can and will, wound and heal, bless and curse.

Circumstantially, they can and will, be absurd, atrocious, vicious, virtuous, arrogant, combative, enlightening, fanatical, fickle, stubborn, insensitive, ridiculous, liberating and imprisoning, loving, comforting, compassionate, consoling, unifying, divisive, reconciliatory, and even constructively transformational and transcendent.

What are we to make of a global entity that presents itself (in a multiplicity of forms), as the *light* to the world, a citadel of *truth*, a trustworthy spiritual *leader,* and reliable *guide* into all the verities and mysteries of spiritual experience, when as a *human collective and global entity*, it becomes *lost* and no longer knows the way? And what exactly has this worldwide spiritual community lost? It has (as will be shown) lost its true *center* and consequently, has lost its *soul*.

CHAPTER TWO
Founders of Religion: The Relational Center

We naturally associate world religions with their founders and/or foundational ideas, teachings, and concepts. To begin to understand religions we must know something about the founders themselves. Upon close examination, we discover what originally compelled, inspired, and motivated them to express what they felt, thought, believed, and lived.

We find, without exception, that all are chiefly concerned about, address, and focus on the *quality or lack thereof of the vital relationships* that shape, inform sustain, (even determine), provide purpose, and give meaning, initially to their own lives, and as expected, to the lives of others. From the beginning, their feelings, thoughts, and experiences *prioritize the matters of relationship in spiritual life, spirituality, and religion*. Their lives, service, messages, missions, endeavors, and enterprises clearly demonstrate *the centrality of relationship in spiritual experience*. Relationship was at the *center* of what can be called the founders *Original*

Spiritual Concern (OSC). In muting, marginalizing, and essentially abandoning the imperatives and implications inherent in the OSC, the GSC has effectively *lost the relational center,* the core of all things spiritual, the unifying thread and center-piece of spiritual experience, and the only *living currency*, if actively apprehended, available to it.

As a collective of individuals and groups, the GSC is a superstructure of multiple, diverse, competing, complimentary, and often confusing, contradicting, antagonistic belief systems. And though often denied, it cannot conceal a most troubling, disturbing, self-inflicted character flaw, which it appears unable and unwilling to extract itself from: *conceptualizing, constructing, and organizing spiritual life, spirituality, and religion to accommodate, advance, and promote its collective and individualized self-interests, which (without exception) are driven, sustained, and fueled by raw self-enhancing, self-indulgent, self-serving, and self-seeking narratives that never sleep.*

This objective assessment will of course be, by many, tenaciously (even angrily) denied, defensively dodged, and vociferously disputed, but, whatever a day may bring forth, never convincingly disproved. The GSC is an entity that may, or may not have, lost its collective mind. But, it has, with heart-breaking consequences, *lost its relational center, the soul of its life.*

Spiritual life, spirituality, and religion do not appear ex nihilo (out of nothing). They emerged from, and within the intimate experience (s) of *relationship.* The global spiritual enterprise and related religious endeavors show a relentless pursuit and consuming concern for the matter of one's relationship to and with who, (and in some cases, what), is perceived as a *Spiritual Referent or Transcendent Spiritual Source.*

It should be kept in mind that in every case, whatever is truly significant in this drama, always occurs within *a constellation of relationships.* Whatever was known, thought, felt, intuited, envisioned, believed, and acted upon, by founders of religion, was, at *the point of origin,* and in the moments of encounter, singularly *relational.* In fact, in the so-called *revealed religions,* whatever came to be known and believed via various forms of *revelation* occurred within the *intimacies of relationship.* Founders were *relationally* encountered and addressed, received messages to proclaim, were appointed messengers, and/or were compelled by, and given a global *relational mission.* They often risked their reputations, lives, family, friends, and fortunes, intrepidly demonstrating by every means available to them, that the matter of relationship (in terms of quality or lack thereof) constitutes the essence of all spiritual experience, expression, and pursuit.

The driving spiritual concern of *founders and reformers* of the principle or major religions of the world, as well as the (so-called) minor religious paths, was unquestionably fueled by a *relational priority.*

Hinduism (ca. 1500 – 4000 B.C.E.), perhaps the world's most multidimensional religion has no human founder, but can be said to have a founding idea/conception (shared by all Hindus) of ultimate reality: the *Brahman*, the "supreme Ground of Being." What is relevant here is that every person and all of existence stands in *relationship* to/with the *Brahman.*

The hymns of the Vedic Age, the Upanishads, Shruti, (words heard) and Smriti, (words remembered) are all perceived among Hindus as revelatory. Essentially, revelation *in and through relationship* with Brahman (the ultimate spiritual reality) is foundational.

In the *bhakti* (The Path of Devotion) tradition of Hinduism, this relationship is intimately personal. It is "a meeting with the divinity" characterized by love, devotion, and service. Once again, the *centrality of relationship* in spiritual experience is the focal point.

Abram [aka Abraham] and Sarai [aka Sarah] (1921 B.C.E.), founding figures in *Judaism* are seen in history as those whom Yahweh *calls,* (Gen. 12), not first and simply to a specific system of belief, theology, and practice, but fundamentally more significant into the intimacies of *relationship*. They were given directions for their ensuing lives and generations to come. God's presence with them and their heirs was not assured by mere words, (words alone are not enough), but emerged from, and resided in a loving, trusting, faithful, obedient, and a *mutually* satisfying, *reciprocal relationship*:

> *Leave your country, your relatives, and*
> *your father's house, and go to the land that*

> *I will show you. I will cause you to become the father of a great nation. I will bless you and make you famous, and I will make you a blessing to others...all the families of the earth will be blessed through you.*

The relational dynamic is also evident in what transpires between Moses and God. God (it is said) considered Moses *a friend* (Exodus 33: 11-23). Genuine friendship is always rooted in a cherished *relationship*.

Christ's invitational, "Follow me" (Mark 2) was, and remains a summons to enter into *relationship.* As the founder and "central figure" of *Christianity*, His clarion call to *"love God with all that you are and your neighbor as yourself"* is an unmistakable *relational mandate*. Saul, (aka Paul), His most ardent disciple and apostle, writes of yet another *relational imperative,* in his incomparable love ethic (Rom. 12):

> *Love is always patient and kind; it is never jealous; love is never boastful or conceited; it is never rude or selfish, it does not take offense, and is not resentful. Love takes no pleasure in other people's sins but delights in truth; it is always ready to*

excuse, to trust, to hope, and to endure whatever comes.

In **Islam,** founded by Muhammad (570 – 632 C.E.), revelation in the realm of relationship comes in the form (an organic and chronological derivative of Judaism), written **Confucianism** thought of as moral, political, and philosophical in nature, founded by K'ung Fu-tzu (551 – 479 BCE) in China, emphasizes *relational* based ethics, virtue, equality, mutuality, and reciprocity (public and private).

Confucius insisted that a well-ordered society was essential for quality **relationships.** This enduring cornerstone of Confucianism is evident in two of his oft-quoted statements: *"What you do not want done to yourself, do not do to others."* And, *"In order to establish oneself, one should try to establish others."*

Revelation in the **realm of relationship** comes in the form of the Qur'an (communicated to Muhammad, its Prophet, by the Angel Gabriel, for Muhammad's recitation and global dissemination.

God "as absolute love" (Al-Wadud) is a major tenet of the **Islamic** faith, along with love's characteristics of mercy and compassion (Ar-Rahman), (11:90, 92). **Muhammad,** prophet of Allah said *"...if you love God, Follow me: and God will love you and forgive you your sins. For God is Oft-forgiving, Most Merciful"* (3:31). Clearly, these beliefs are expressed in the **spirit and language of relationship.**

Philosophical and religious in nature, **Buddhism** (6th century B.C.E.) addresses the human suffering and provides a course of action in response to this universal phenomenon. Buddhism explores suffering in terms of its cause and effect, and how one can respond to this common human experience.

The founder, **Siddhartha Gautama** (581 -501 B.C.E.), **the Buddha** observing both suffering and death, (and their causation), reached a point in his own spiritual development that would frame his responsive mission, message and a method for remedy. His instruction to disciples was *"Go forth, O Bhikkus (monks) for the benefit of many, for the bliss of many, out of compassion for the world."*

An empathetic **compassion** for *all* is a hallmark of Buddhism. And compassion only happens in community and within **relationship**. There is no question that the Buddha's motivation was immersed in, and driven by an immense **relational concern.**

In the Analects of Confucius (referred to above), we also find his counsel, "Do not do to others what you would not like yourself. Then there will be no resentment against you, either in the family or in the state." What are family and state realities, if not about the actual **relationships** they invoke?

The **Sikh** faith – founded by Nanak Dev Ji (1469 – 1539 C.E.), its first guru – also has an inside track when it comes to its conscious emphasis on **relationships**. The name **Sikh** is a derivative of Sikha and means "disciple." Its founder, Guru Nanak (1469-1539) of Pakistan, strikes a characteristic note of intimate **relationship** between God and humanity in the statement *"Search not for the True One afar off; He is in every heart, and is known by the Guru's instruction."* This active sense of universal equality amongst all people is accompanied by a heightened sense of service in community, *"Me, a bard out of work, the Lord has applied me to his service."*

These *relational emphases* find themselves firmly rooted in a spiritual framework that recognizes the *centrality of relationship*. The *relational content, character, and context* at the heart of still other religious traditions, spiritual paths, and interests (First Peoples, African, African-American, Hispanic, Women etc.), will not go un-noted and will be explored in a subsequent chapter.

The point to be made in highlighting what motivated *founders and reformers of religions,* is that without exception, all, representing a multiplicity of religious/spiritual faiths, paths, and traditions, began with an *emphatic* concern, interest, and care for the improvement, enhancement, and enrichment of life's most basic and essential *relationships*. In all the annals of spiritual experience, people world-over (past and present) serve as a testament and witness to the incontestable truth, that everything spiritual, finds its *genesis, continuation, and completion in the realm of relationship.*

Founders of religion did not come to realize the *centrality of relationship* in spiritual experience through their own human genius, wisdom, and insight. They put their emphasis on relationships simply because real life is all about relationships (all types and kinds).

CHAPTER THREE
This Thing Called Life: The Sum of Our Relationships

What, in the end, is life, if not the sum of our relationships? Founders of religions understood experientially, this simple, yet fundamental axiom. Their approaches and perspectives on anything and everything involving spiritual life, spirituality, and religion, strove to be in harmony with, attuned to, and reflective of this truth, **personally, socially, organizationally, and institutionally.**

The GSC is negligent and deficient in this respect. It has walked away, moved off of, and consequently *lost the relational center* that founders of religion constructed their religious consciousness around. From womb to tomb, blissful, blessed, blistering, or broken, joyful, sorrowful or despairing, midst tension, stress and anxiety, exasperation or exhilaration, in health or illness, at every stage of existence, life (collectively and individually) is an experience in relationship.

Jungian analyst, Eleanor Bertine M.D., addressing the determinative force and power of relationships, rightly notes:

Some problem of human relationship is the immediate cause that brings many to consult an analyst. In the privacy of the consulting room a multitude of such difficulties are revealed. Whether the relation is one of friend, lover, business associate, or enemy, it has the power to bring joy, sorrow, anxiety, and despair.

Further, she is well aware that:

> It is possible to develop a certain amount of consciousness in relation to things and inanimate nature, and even more in relation to animals, where feeling may be strongly touched. But only another human being can constellate so many sides of ourselves, can react so pointedly, and can bring to consciousness so much of which we had been unaware.

Many (religious and secular) uniformly fail to grasp, and constructively act on this unassailable law of life, the GSC can least afford to do so.

As if to magnify its *relational plight*, C.G. Jung's psycho-spiritual insight (which can serve as an aid to the GSC) aptly describes its familiar/unfamiliar, approach/avoid approach to, and comprehension of, the significance of relationship in spiritual experience, counseling that *"We must admit that what is closest to us is the very thing we know least about, although, it seems to be what we know best of all."*

The GSC *assents* to the proposition, and *agrees* with the truth, that relationships are *central and at the core* of spiritual experience. But assent and agreement are not enough, and are no cause for celebration, as they engage the mind but not always the heart, and offer no actionable assurances or prospects that demonstrations are certain to follow.

Rather than reflecting, embracing, and concentrating its collective might and powers on enhancing, improving, and enriching *relationships* (near and far), its agendas are elsewhere.

The GSC, as a collective consisting of people in all religions and every faith), is less concerned with/for *actual relationships,* and more concerned with:

1) whose doctrines are right, purest, trustworthy, or most orthodox, 2) whose theology is most fundamental, conservative, centrist, progressive, eclectic, radical, or revolutionary, practical, oldest or newest 3) whose religious tradition is most hallowed, noteworthy, and best, 4) whose spirituality is most pious, moral, ethical, rational, contemplative, meditative, mystical, or esoteric, 5) whose spiritual or religious philosophy is wisest, practical, or most relevant, 6) whose religious laws are most humane, merciful, just, and righteous 7) whose religious principles and practices are most glorious and sublime, 8) whose creeds, rituals, rites, sacraments, and symbols are most meaningful, and of course, 9) whose religion, spiritual path, or movement is closest to who or what is deemed the ultimate transcendent Source. An active concern, concrete engagement, and the passionate prioritization of *actual relationships* does not even make the list.

At the intersection of *religion and politics,* the *relational priority* is similarly *jettisoned* by the GSC. Here too, it prefers to relentlessly focus on, and strenuously emphasize:

1) what or whose culture is superior, definitive, absolute 2) whose economic system is most beneficial and/or best, 3) whose form of government is advantageous and/or most advanced, whose political philosophies and perspectives are best and most suitable for life 3) who is wisest, wealthiest or most powerful, and 5) whose color, tribe, nationality, language, ethnicity, gender, sexuality, age, class, caste, or social status is construed as best, superior, preferable, or worst. The actual quality or lack thereof of relationships, from which all of the above experiences emerge, rates less than a footnote.

This ***relational obliviousness*** stands in the face of the obvious fact that all persons and things exist within an interconnected universe consisting of relationships (all types and kinds). An incomprehensible disconnect (that one would naturally expect only of a corpse), from the moral-spiritual imperatives and compelling socio-ethical implications implicit in the most obvious of truths: there is no life (spiritual or otherwise) in the absence of relationship.

How does the GSC manage to overlook this universal truth? In exploring the statement, "what makes sense of our experience" Anthony Storr, author of *Solitude: A Return to the Self* writes:

> We are, as it were, embedded in a structure of which unique relationships are the supporting pillars. We take this so much for granted that we seldom define it, and may hardly be conscious of it until some important relationship comes to an end.

In his reflection Storr shows how, even in terms of relationships dearest to us, we can go unconscious as to their inestimable significance. And alas, things happen, events transpire, situations arise, and waking us up, to their value and their impact on/in the lives we live. Has the GSC gone **relationally unconscious**?

Is it as Pascal (1623 – 1662) once said, because "First principles are too self-evident for us." Or, perhaps, as Bertrand Russell (1872- 1970) observed two centuries later, is it a case of "...something so simple, as not to seem worth stating." Whatever the case or reason, the **centrality of relationship** in spiritual life, spirituality, and religion remains at the heart of spiritual experience. And it is not fatalistic, hype, or exaggeration to assert that (more than any other single factor) **our relationships** (their quality or lack thereof) determine the content, course, direction and outcome of our lives.

CHAPTER FOUR
Life: The Gold Standard of Spiritual Experience

Why are *relationships* the gold standard of spiritual experience? And why should the GSC, (as individuals and groups) *put relationships first*, in the life-altering experiences of *spiritual life, spirituality, and religion*? It should do so because *life is the sum of our relationships.* The answer is both astonishingly simple and profoundly complex, yet easily substantiated.

In and through *relational experiences* we find:

- Meaning and purpose
- Contentment and fulfillment
- Love and belonging
- Happiness and hope,
- Joy and satisfaction
- Oneself and other selves
- Acceptance and rejection
- Faults and flaws,
- Betrayals and losses
- Possibilities and limitations
- Sadness and suffering
- Illness and disease
- Health and healing
- Tranquility and turmoil

- Failure and defeat
- Adversity and triumph
- Grief and despair
- Agony and ecstasy
- Guilt, grace, forgiveness, reconciliation and gratitude
- Remorse and recrimination
- Wholeness and fragmentation
- Dislocation and distress
- Frustration and futility
- Fear, anger and anxiety
- Transgression and alienation
- Remorse and recrimination
- Judgment and condemnation
- Oppression or liberation
- Cultures and civilizations
- Ideals, virtues and values
- Challenges and obstacles
- Courage, doubt and cowardice
- Shame and embarrassment
- Morality and ethics
- Sexuality and sex
- Wisdom and folly
- Truth, power and justice
- Chaos and concord
- War and peace
- Life and death

In and through relationship we experience whether we are:

- Wanted or unwanted
- Enough or not
- Loved or unloved
- Recognized or neglected
- Protected or unprotected
- Honored and valued, or degraded and discounted
- Validated or invalidated

The psycho-spiritual, emotional, and physical wounds we receive and/or cause occur in the context of our relationships:

- Husbands and wives
- Fathers and mothers
- Sons and daughters
- Brothers and sisters
- Extended relatives
- Friends and enemies
- Couples, companions and partners
- Social, educational, civic, legal and governmental institutions/agencies.

Life: In Review and Reflection

The centrality of relationship in the whole of one's life is easy to show and easily confirmed in a reflective review of our individual lives (past and present). We are born in and through our parent's relationship. What were our first years like? Were we welcomed, received, touched, held and care for (or not) in these first relationships? Who told us who we were, who they were, and the meaning of family and home?

If we did not live with both parents, we lived with one. If we lived with neither, we lived with someone (in relationship) at some time, somewhere, in some way. What happened and how we felt in these first relationships affected us to such a degree as to leave an indelible impression upon us that lasts a lifetime.

Reviewing and reflecting on our first relationships allows us to ask, how did mom and/or dad and others treat me? Why was I so treated? Who was present with/for me, who was not? Did I feel safe, secure and protected? Who was I able to trust?

Was life calm, serene and stable or chaotically random and unpredictable? Was I frightened and endangered, abused and/or abandoned? Who could I count on or not? What did or did not, my first relationships teach me? How did I see the world through them? When did I first have a feel for, or sense of, the God or a transcendent spiritual source?

What were my experiences in subsequent years? Who and what brought me joy? What hurt, saddened and disappointed me? Who encouraged and spoke to me of my talents, gifts potential and possibilities? Who knew and empathized with my struggles and my pain? Who saw me weep, cried with me and wiped my tears away? Who took time and showed my positive concern, interest and understanding?

What were my trials, tests, and challenges in adolescence, youth and young adulthood? Who affirmed and supported me through them, who cared? What has happened in my life since entering adulthood? What has become of my hopes, wishes, ambitions, ideals and dreams? What have been and remain the watershed experiences of my life? How have I been psycho-spiritually and emotional effected by the sum of my experiences to this point in my life? What is happening now and what is before me?

Other questions may move to the center of our concerns. Who or what is God? Do I have a spiritual identity? If so, what is it? Is God present in my relationships? Why do spiritual life, spirituality and religion frequently promise much but disappointingly often deliver so little? To what extent does spirituality encourage my experiences and processes of self-awareness, self-knowledge, self-understanding and self-discovery?

Why do conventional religion, religious conformity and the religious status quo resist and object to vitally new vistas, broader views and a deepened understanding and experience of spiritual growth and development? Why does religion often destroy rather than create, impair rather than improve, impoverish rather than enrich, diminish rather than enhance and wound rather than heal? What significance does spiritual life have in relation to world issues and events? What roles and responsibilities do those in positions of spiritual leadership have in community life and global affairs?

Do spiritual life, spirituality and religion open up or close down possibilities and prospects of authentic healing in regard to my psycho-spiritual-emotional wounds? Am I working with God and others toward a healing wholeness within myself and in my relations with others?

An authentic review and a realistic reflection of our lives reveal a picture of relationships. The whole of our living experience, from the very beginning, occurred (and continues) within a **constellation of relationships.**

Our lives are healthiest, happiest, and most fulfilling to the degree that we actively devote our best energies in tending to, and caring for, all of the relationships that constitute and sustain the lives *we* and *others* live.

The universal question commonly asked, **how** can we do this or that, is understandable and necessary, but should not be the first one we seek an answer to. The initial and more profound questions are **what** does it require, and **who** must one become?

CHAPTER FIVE
Spiritual Life, Spirituality, and Religion: First Things

To put something first, we prioritize it. We consciously choose to make something more important, significant, and valuable than something else.

Loyal adherents, committed followers within all the faiths, traditions, paths, and movements that constitute the GSC, make decisions and act upon what is deemed to be of first order in spiritual experience. All, without exception, engage in various forms of prioritization.

Determining and embracing what matters most and what we shall put first is an often exacting, but indispensable endeavor. In the process, we explore and ask what is it that must be prioritized? What is central? What matters most? What shall be in the forefront? What is our primary point of reference, guiding principle, point of departure and specific destination? What, after all, is the chief concern or essence of spiritual life, spirituality, and religion? What is decisive for us? What do we put first? Why have we put it first, and how are we actively demonstrating this priority?

Wolman (2001:119), in his book, (*Thinking with Your Soul*) recognizes the experience and process of prioritization:

> Each of us makes personal and intimate choices about what we value, whom we love, what we are willing to devote our lives to, and what form our relationship to transcendent phenomenon can take. In this manner, we shape our individual spiritual relationships to the world.

Prioritization is universal. Groups within the GSC are known and easily identified by their particular interests, considerations and concerns. Individuals and groups invariably reach decisions and commonly make choices as to what is put first (in terms of values, principles, endeavors, enterprises, programs, and practices) among many competing (often conflicting) alternatives. The work of prioritization involves deliberation, choice and decision. In the process, some things will inevitably fall away, or be eliminated, while others will be kept as first-order, non-negotiable essentials. Every individual, all groups, every "version" of spiritual experience within the GSC (conscious or not), engages in some form of prioritization. There is always a spiritual hierarchy that indicates what is felt to matter most in spiritual experience. How the GSC does this is easily shown.

Pseudo-Spiritual Priorities: Corridors and Pathways of Diversion, Distraction, Division, Deflection, and Destruction

As to pseudo-spiritual priorities, alone, one of them can disturb and disrupt. Converging, they present the perfect spiritual storm.

"Conventional Spirituality": The Conventional Priority

Conventional Spirituality is a classic example of the universal tendency of many individuals and groups to conform their respective faiths and religions to the prevailing self-serving, self-seeking interests of nation, state, tribe, class, gender, ethnicity, language, polity, and whatever happens to be the operative status quo.

Advocates and proponents in the GSC of *conventional spirituality,* summarily put customs, traditions and community consensus first. There is a sheepish conformity to the values, dictates, desires and wishes of most everything that is conventionally accepted and approved. Adherents and followers are conveniently at ease and comfortable with going along and getting along with the dominant interests of the socio-cultural-political order in which they comfortably find themselves.

An illuminating case in point is the 1963 story surrounding Dr. Martin Luther King's famous letter from a Birmingham, Alabama jail. A white ecumenical ministerial alliance (Catholic, Jewish, Episcopal, Methodist, Baptist, and Presbyterian) wrote and submitted a letter entitled "A Call for Unity" to Birmingham newspaper.

Supporting the prevailing racial status quo, social conventions and community customs (white supremacy/superiority, black subservience/inferiority, inequitable segregation, and sanctioned racial discrimination), the white ecumenical clergy alliance strongly objected to demonstrations for civil rights, social justice, freedom, equality and liberty by King and his associates arguing that: "we are convinced that these demonstrations are unwise and untimely."

"A Call for Unity" was a call to convention and conformity, a religious defense by the white religious establishment of the customary system of white socio-cultural supremacy and political dominance. It was an immoral and unjust system of "white over black" that made citywide non-violent civil disobedience in Birmingham, Alabama inevitable. King's transcendent prophetic reply "Letter from a Birmingham jail" on the other hand, was a positive psycho-socio-spiritual and political mandate designed to enrich, enhance and improve (in a word, heal) a community engulfed and entrenched in discord, division, enmity, anger, hatred and strife.

King's 1963, Letter from a Birmingham Jail silenced the tepid white ecumenical conventional clergy signatories of the "Call to Unity" letter reminding them that:

> There was a time when the church was very powerful...In those days the church was not merely a thermometer that recorded the ideas and principles of popular opinion; it was a thermostat that transformed the mores of society...Things are different now. So often the contemporary church is a weak, ineffectual voice with an uncertain sound. So often it is arch-defender of the status quo...Is organized religion too inextricably bound to

the status quo to save our nation and the world? Perhaps I must turn my faith to the inner spiritual church, the church within the church, as the true ekklesia and the hope of the world.

Conventional spirituality (putting convention first) leads to a twisted and entangled conformity (often to the worst aspects of a given social order). It always mars and disfigures the best in spiritual life, spirituality and religion. It's likely that Jung (1958: 336, 337) had conventional spirituality in mind (and were he alive today, would have used gender inclusive language), when in the 50's he said:

I have found that modern man has an aversion for traditional opinions and inherited truths...all spiritual standards and forms of the past have somehow lost their vitality...confronted with this attitude, every ecclesiastical system finds itself in an awkward situation, be it Catholic, Protestant, Buddhist or Confucianist...exceptionally able, courageous and upright persons who repudiate traditional truths for honest and decent reasons, and not from wickedness of heart...everyone of them has the feeling that our religious truths have somehow become hollow...have lost their authority and psychological justification.

Wherever and whenever it prevails, *conventional spirituality* (in any of its chameleon guises) is a complete hindrance to spiritual progress for any individual or group.

"Intellectual Spirituality": The Intellectual Priority

As briefly mentioned earlier, but now more precisely, some put the intellect first, developing an *"intellectual spirituality"* that prioritizes the intellect. The mental formation, construction and content of spiritual life are the dominant feature. It is nothing less than a *rationalization* of spiritual experience.

In assessing "intellectual spirituality" it is beneficial to clarify and distinguish some other very important matters.

"Thought" and "Thinking"

There is a distinction between "breath" and "breathing" (all living persons require oxygen and breath, but breathing (inhaling and exhaling) is individualized, occurring at differing degrees of rate, pace, and depth). In similar fashion, there is also a distinction between "thought" and "thinking." They are analogous to breath and breathing. Thought and thinking are unitary but not synonymous. An intellectual orientation (as an example) is simply a particular approach to, or type of thinking (among multiple other "thinking orientations"). Alone and isolation, it does not represent **the nature of thought**. Thinking "orientations," "processes" and "pattern" are the **products** of Thought.

In other words, "thought" is an inherent human attribute and activity, a universal human capacity, comprised of many elements (feeling, contemplation reflection, intuition, meditation, retrospection, projection, fore and after-thought, memory and imagination etc.).

Everyone, everywhere, engages in *"thought,"* but all people do not *"think"* alike, in the same manner or about the same things. Thought, (in its most complete sense) is not exclusive to the West. However, "how" the West thinks, is peculiarly western. Thought then, is an *attribute,* while thinking is a *process.* Life experiences (where our feet are planted) determine *how* we think (process) and *what* we think (content).

In an economy of words, thought is a universal human attribute while thinking is universally particularistic, informed and shaped by the convergent experiences of culture, geography, language, and even temperament. In regard to spiritual life, spirituality and religion, I view the attribute of, and capacity for *Thought* as divinely derived.

Theology and Spiritual Experience

A word about theology and spiritual experience is in order here. Theology and spiritual experience are not synonyms. Theology, as known in the West (Europe, North America, Australia, and related geographical/cultural satellites), is typically an academic enterprise, devised in academia, by and principally for the academy.

Western theologies are crafted and systematized as intellectual endeavors, taught in educational venues (classroom and lecture halls) for transmission to a multiplicity of culturally and educationally diverse faith communities.

Traditional theologies (as orderly systematized compendiums of religious thinking) are purely mental constructs, principally preoccupied with concepts, ideas and theories **_"about"_** relations between and among human beings and their referential transcendent spiritual sources (known and called, world-wide, by many names, in various languages).

Conventional theological studies culminate in the attainment of educational degrees and professional positions. *Relationships* do not. All attempts to comprehend spiritual life, spirituality and religion principally through theological words, concepts and ideas, severely handicap the religiously inclined and spiritually engaged.

The concerns of authentic spiritual life engage and involve so much more (as in the real lives of actual people, experiences and concrete situations). By its very nature, spiritual life is what we continuously and more meaningfully experience long before and far beyond the limited speculative rationalistic interest, considerations and concerns of the academic/intellectual theological enterprise. The depth, detail and passion of spiritual life cannot be felt/known when cuffed by, and confined to mere "theology."

Traditional theological questions, issues and models of the West, have, for some time, been and remain, in varying states of exhaustion and impotency, with little left to offer in the new arenas of spiritual life in the 21st century. Though maintaining its current military, economic, scientific and technological advantages, the West, at the same time, is an unreliable and untrustworthy guide in the vital matters and essential concerns of spiritual life, spirituality, and religion. Over against the common and very ordinary "rationalistic approach," spirituality today, requires and demands a *"relational turn."*

None of this should be construed as an attempt to frame theological endeavor and living relationships as antagonistic or mutually exclusive polarities. R/S has no interest and does not engage in such wrangling.

In R/S, spiritual truths are realized and authenticated, not by the logic of particularistic theologies or other noetic spiritual orientations, but in the specificities of real persons and groups in the contexts of their actual relationships (not simply within, but also beyond their immediate circles and circumscribed zones of comfortability).

Written and verbal abstractions are more important (valued more highly), in "intellectual spirituality" than the necessity and need of experiential actualization. The pursuit and acquisition of knowledge in terms words, ideas, concepts, systems, data and information make the *centrality of the intellect* the ruling religious value.

Failing (lacking the ability) to integrate, harmonize and unite mental capacity with the other natural faculties that constitute a whole human being *(i.e. the psycho-spiritual, intuitive, emotional, physical),* one is left out in the cold, with life-less spiritual abstraction, masquerading as spiritual profundity.

C. G. Jung clinically disrobes and exposes the psychological nakedness of the "intellectual" priority, (what he says relative to psychology applies to spiritual experience as well):

> It is precisely our experiences in psychology which demonstrate as plainly as could be wished that the intellectual "grasp"

of a psychological fact produces no more than a concept…In psychology one possesses nothing unless one has experienced it in reality. Hence a purely intellectual insight is not enough, because one knows only the words and not the substance of the thing from the inside.

Jung makes himself entirely clear on this point noting that:

Nothing influences our conduct less than intellectual ideas…Mere talk has always been considered hollow and there is no trick, however cunning, by which one can evade this simple rule for long. The fact of being convinced, and not the subject matter of conviction, it is this which has always carried the weight.

Martin Buber, another spiritual luminary writes (1958: 11, 13) that:

No system of ideas, no foreknowledge, and no fancy intervene between I and Thou…Appeal to a "world of ideas" will not do away with its you and of me, of our life, and our world – not of and I or a state of being, in itself alone. The real boundary for the actual man cuts right across the world of ideas as well.

We do not disagree that "Intellectual Spirituality" is strong in that which involves "religious/theological analysis, but it is outrageously weak, knows nothing, and offers nothing, that is actually *relationally attuned and immersed in relational concerns.* In substance, it is empathetically incapable of getting beyond its original dynamic: the *depersonalization and abstraction* of life. As in Plato, ideas (things of the mind) are all it knows and what matters most.

There is no room for real people and their *actual relationships*, which are about, and have everything to do with the concrete realities and experiences of real life, real feelings, real joys and real pain. Wherever *Intellectual Spirituality* (putting the intellect first) dominates, one finds a titanic block to a therapeutic, unified, and beneficent spiritual experience.

"Ecclesiastical Spirituality": The Ecclesiastical Priority

Another spiritual impediment common to the religiously inclined and spiritually engaged (especially in every established faith and spiritual path) is **ecclesiastical spirituality.** Here, as stated earlier, spiritual life is not liberating and transformational, but bound and confined to the *self-serving/self-seeking interests* of a single religious group or spiritual movement.

Among these groups, (at all costs) the first concern and primary focus is on self-preservation, promotion, continuity, justification and defense of its own peculiar sense of religious completion or spiritual finality.

The ultimate in spiritual life is *their* spiritual perspective or religious system. Religious leaders and followers believe and behave as though they represent the truest of orthodoxies *of and for* all time. To question this (especially as an insider) is considered an anathema, borders on heresy and incurs considerable wrath. And when not vigilantly restrained, can lead to the imposition of death.

Tolstoy's public writings and pronouncements (often denouncing the mutually aggrandizing self-serving behavior of both church and state) critiqued and challenged ecclesiastical spirituality prevalent in his own tradition (the Russian Orthodox Church). The official response to Tolstoy was excommunication. He was charged as having:

> ...led astray by pride...boldly and indolently dared to oppose God, Christ, and his holy heirs...denied the mother who nurtured him and brought him up: the Orthodox Church...undermining the Orthodox Church, which upholds the universe, in which our ancestors lived and were saved and in which Holy Russia has remained strong until this day. In his works and letters, circulated in great numbers throughout the world...he preaches the abolition of all the dogma of the Orthodox Church.

Tolstoy makes his assessment and evaluation of the Russian Orthodox Church, and other traditions engaged in ecclesiastical spirituality, indelibly clear:

> The churches are everywhere the same...every church, in so far as it is a church, cannot but strive for the same object as the Russian Church. That object is to conceal the real meaning of Christ teachings and to replace it by their own, which lays no obligation on them and excludes the possibility of understanding the true teaching of Christ...There is the same external ritual...the same loftily vague discussions of

Christianity in books and sermons, and when it comes to practice, the same supporting of the present idolatry...There is always the same activity directed to concealing the real duties of Christianity, and putting in their place an external respectability and cant.

Ecclesiastical Spirituality is the Achilles' heel of every established religion/spiritual path found in the annals of history and in today's media. If, in relation to ecclesiastical spirituality, you bet that all spiritually progressive steps forward are generally followed by two steps backwards or side-ways, you will most often hold the winning hand.

"Group Spirituality": The Group Priority

Group life, as we know, is a universal phenomenon. On the American scene, Nathan Glazer, reminds us that the "Peoples of America" consist of many ethnically self-conscious groups:

> ...Since the end of European mass immigration to this country...we have waited for the subsidence of ethnic self-consciousness, and often announced it, and it has returned again and again. But each time it has returned in so different a form...

Harold Cruse, *The Crisis of the Negro Intellectual* similarly recognized the phenomenon of group identity and affiliation in American life noting that Americans live in a society whose:

> ...legal Constitution recognizes the rights, privileges and aspirations of the individual, but whose political institutions recognize the reality of ethnic groups...that America, which idealizes the rights of the individual above everything else, is in reality, a nation dominated by the social power of groups, classes, in-groups and cliques – both ethnic and religious. The individual in America has few rights that are not backed up by the political, economic and social power of one group or another...each individual American is a member of a group.

If Cruse and Glazer (both ethnic Americans, African and Jewish respectively) have a point, then the likelihood of making spiritual life, spirituality, and religion subservient to group interests, needs, wants, and desires is a real and present danger.

The collective spiritual life (life in a faith community or spiritual path) exhibits all of the signs commonly observed in groups considered secular. There is no pleasant spin for this. At the end of the day, the matter is plain, each, driven by self-seeking self-interests, simply go for what is wanted for itself, others be damned.

In this regard, Reinhold Niebuhr, in his book, *Moral Man and Immoral Society*, cutting to the bone, assures us of the following, with irrefutable clarity:

> ...the group which organizes any society, however social its intention or pretentions, arrogates an inordinate portion of social privilege to itself...The fact that the hypocrisy of man's group behavior...expresses itself not only in terms of self-justification of human behavior in general, symbolizes one of the tragedies of the human spirit; its inability to conform its collective life to its...ideals...As racial, economic and national groups they take for themselves, whatever their power can command.

In the totality of the matter, consider **group spirituality** as the commander-in chief of spiritual prioritization, and conventional, intellectual, and ecclesiastical priorities as standing reinforcements.

At the start, it must be said that group identity (affinity and association) are obviously vital components of life and ought never be disparaged or devalued. That is, until they misbehave (as when they become self-serving, self-seeking, self-absorbed, hardened and without active positive regard for the well-being of other groups that constitute the human family.

Group Spirituality can be readily detected and easily exposed. A group embraces a particular religion, **strains** it through *a **pre-existing** **self-set*** of psychological, temperamental, cultural, ethnic, tribal, gender, sexuality, cultural, educational, political, class, status, caste, socio-economic, (and come lately, racial) **filters,** until a finely **distilled** creation takes shape, emerges, and crystalizes into, what now becomes identified (which it is not), the **essence** of the religion or faith, the group initially received and embraced. At which point, the religion and the group's self-interests become indistinguishably, one and the same. The religion has been tailored and exclusively designed to promote **a group-self-serving conception of Divinity and a corresponding spiritual universe that suits only itself, its interests, and its concerns.**

Putting "the group" first, plays itself out in a number of horrific global religious, ethnic, socio-political-economic and military conflicts.

1) The war in former Yugoslavia (1991- 1995) where Orthodox Serbian Christians, Catholic Croat Christians, and Bosnian Muslims (each exclusively devoted to the preservation and transmission of their own group "interests" by any means necessary) became engulfed in war, *"ethnic cleansing,"* mass murder, rape, mutilation, retaliatory vengeance and terror.

(2) In the 1994 Rwanda civil war, a conflict between two tribal groups (Tutsis and Hutus) brought into play by Belgian imperial colonialism (1901-1962), 800,000 to one million men, women, and children lost their lives, land, and possessions.

All parties were at least nominally Christian and identified with Catholicism. Was this a redemptive demonstration of the self-less "kingdom of God" by any of these groups, or flat-out examples of the self-seeking, self-serving, self-interests of national, ethnic and tribal kingdoms? When groups (especially religious) put themselves first, spiritual beliefs and values are always the first to go.

(3) The Northern Ireland conflict (involving Irish Catholics and English Protestants, 1968-present) has left approximately 3,700 deaths and related losses. Each group historically and traditionally embraced Christianity of a type that had no observable bearing on their respective destructive behaviors. The conflict, begun by 17th century English imperialism continues to fester today.

(4) The conflict involving Israeli Jews and Palestinian Arabs, stemming from a 7th century Arab invasion of Palestine (home to the Jews of that era). Stretching further back in time, the story of this matter is long and complex. What is certain is that it clearly involves two groups differing in religion, culture, language, tribal identities and ethnic affiliations. The religious traditions, ideals, and values of both groups (combined with geo-political interests) fuel and sustain, rather than ameliorate carnage, destruction, misery and mayhem. Religious, values ideals and standards of justice and peace are jettisoned, making justice and peace impossible to attain.

Group inter-religious conflicts, intra-religious rivalries, coupled with ethnic grievances, disputes, and political partisanship are global contemporary realities on every continent (Africa, Asia, Europe, North America, South America, Australia, Antarctica, as well as Islands of the sea). Most anywhere on the globe, groups staunchly justify and defend themselves, and their positions. The powers that be (usually unjust), ostensibly, seem to be winning at this game. Yet, that all depends on how one understand, comprehends, and defines 'winning."

In this inequitable equation, where groups are embroiled, engulfed, and enslaved in "group first" feelings, attitudes and behaviors, peace has no chance. The transcendentalist, Ralph Waldo Emerson addresses (from his own experiences), a different set of religious concerns. His feelings and thoughts on religion continue to attract attention, he believed that:

> Religion is the emotion of reverence, which the presence of the universal mind ever excites in the individual. Now the first position I make is that natural religion supplies still all the facts which are disguised under the dogma of popular creeds...In

religion, the sentiment is all; the ritual or ceremony indifferent...the creeds are outgrown; a technical theology no longer suits us...religion is the relation of the soul to God...sectarianism marks the decline of religion...In the Bible you are not directed to be a Unitarian, or a Calvinist or an Episcopalian... Socrates, Aristotle, Calvin, Luther, Abelard, what are these but names of parties? Which is to say, we quit these parties or Unthinking Corporation, and join ourselves to God in an unpartaken relation.

With profound (near unmatched) insight, Leo Tolstoy, who needs no introduction, (War and Peace, Anna Karenina, The Kingdom of God is Within You), analyzed the politics of the Russian State and the religion of the Russian Orthodox Church in his native Russia, arriving (in 1894) at the following assessment:

Not without good reason was Christ's only harshest and threatening reproof directed against hypocrites and hypocrisy. It is not theft nor robbery nor murder nor fornication, but falsehood, the special falsehood of hypocrisy, which corrupts...those who know the truth and do evil masked by hypocrisy, injure themselves and their victims, and thousands of other men as well who are led astray by the falsehood with which the wrongdoing is disguised. Thieves, robbers, murderers, and cheats, who commit crimes recognized by themselves and everyone else as evil, serve as an example of what ought not to be done, and deter others from similar crimes.

But those who commit the same thefts, robberies, murders, and other crimes, disguising them under all kinds of religious or scientific or humanitarian justifications, as all landowners, merchants, manufactures, and government officials do, provoke others to imitation, and so do harm not only to those who are directly the victims of their crimes, but to the thousands and millions of men whom they corrupt by obliterating their of the distinction between right and wrong.

One immediately sees why a religion of this sort, ensnared by **Group Spirituality**, disqualifies itself, and has no authentic claim or genuine credibility *as a universal religion for all people.* From beginning to end, the primary focus and driving impetus is on *self-serving, self-seeking* group interests, considerations, and concerns, making it incapable of equitable relationships of respect, mutuality and reciprocity in relation to others. It's religious views and perspectives are closed. They may not be reviewed, examined, revised, questioned, or challenged without reprisal. In all aspects of spiritual experience, the interests of the group (vile or virtuous) are decisive, presumptuously absolute, and final. Communities in the world of authentic religion and genuine faith (the GSC), ought not express, exhibit, or participate in such destructive narcissistic vanity.

With respect to *the relational priority in spiritual experience,* individual members and groups within the GSC must critically explore and examine each *one's own religion*, and set forth that faiths', and/or, one's individual response, to the *centrality of relationship* in the arenas of that religion's actual behaviors and practices.

Full Disclosure: Authentic Self-Critique, Criticism, and Assessment of One's Own Religion, Faith, Spiritual Path, or Movement

On the way to recovering the *relational center* of spiritual experience, the GSC, will not get there, if individual members, looking for an easy solution to this problem through a quick fix, recoil and avoid the exacting processes of self-scrutiny and assessment of their respective faiths.

By way of testimonial, as to my own particular faith, I will, by example, follow my own *disclosure counsel*. I am *a follower of Christ*; I take my cues from Him. I do not identify with, and make every possible effort to not associate myself with the *nomenclatures*, "Christian or Christianity." They most always (historically and contemporarily), suggest un-Christ-like, affinity and associations with this or that sub-culture, political ideology, and social perspective inimical to everything there is to be known about the historical Christ of Scripture.

In my view, the content, pictures, and images these words conjure up and present a *fabricated/manufactured Christ*, malleable to serve all manner of self-serving persons, groups, and interests that, in no way, represent Christ, and are sinisterly contrary and antithetical to the clearly revealed *socio- moral, and ethically redemptive values, he offers (non-coercively), to a world in extreme need of them.*

To speak of Christianity, and claim that one is Christian (without further clarification) is ambiguous and confusing. Both terms are nondescript. Alone, they tell us next to nothing and offer no clarity in regard to "what", "who", "how", "when", and "where", or "which one", "what kind", "by what means", and to "what ends"? Both have earned a hard-to-evade reputation of fomenting and/or colluding with a lot of dark stuff.

No, first and foremost, I identify, associate, and align myself with Christ and what he's done and does, and disassociate myself from the perennial ***Christian Affliction*** (which few escape), that just doesn't go away: Coming to Christ as he is, and commencing to make him, who, and what, he is not.

W.E.B. Dubois (noted African-American scholar, author, sociologist, and socio-cultural political commentator/activist) reflects on religion and significant aspects of his personal experiences. It appears as though, he had some of these Christian "afflictions" in mind, noting in his autobiography that:

My religious development has been slow and uncertain. I grew up in a liberal Congregational Sunday School and listened once a week to sermons on doing good as a reasonable duty. Theology played a minor part...At 17 I was in a missionary college where religious orthodoxy was stressed. My "morals" were sound, even a bit puritanical, but when a hidebound old deacon inveighed against dancing I rebelled.

By the time of graduation, I was still a "believer" in orthodox religion, but had strong questions which were encouraged at Harvard. In Germany I became a freethinker and when I came to teach at an Orthodox Methodist Negro school I was soon regarded with suspicion.

When I became head of a department in Atlanta...I was using Crapsey's Religion and Politics as a Sunday School text. When Crapsey was hauled up for heresy, I refused further to teach Sunday school. When my archdeacon Henry Phillips, my last rector died, I flatly refused again to join any church or Sign any church creed. From my 30th year on, I have increasingly regarded the church as an institution which defended such evils as slavery, caste color, exploitation of labor and war.

Christ as Relational

Many in the Christian sector of the GSC, marginalize, mute, ignore, and when it advances their interests, simply abandon **Christ's relational concern.** Yet, the concern for relationships (their quality or lack thereof) is at the center of Christ's life, teachings, message and mission. He embodies and demonstrates a comprehensive spiritual paradigm that is concretely demonstrated in, and through, **redemptive and redeeming relationships.** Words, concepts, and systems may point to spiritual truths, but only **actual relationships provide verifiable confirmation.**

In disposition, character, demeanor and behavior, Christ affirms the three fundamental pillars of spiritual experience (first chapter). He shows that **Spiritual life** is the reality and natural experience of spiritual beings (which we, as humans uniquely are). He knows that **Spirituality** (in its multiple and diverse forms) is the way or manner in which individuals and groups express spiritual life. On the other hand, he saw **religion** (organized, unorganized, re-organized, disorganized, institutional, old or new) not as the **source,** but a *reflection* (a product if you will) of spiritual life. And **Spiritual experience** (comprehensively speaking) is the sum of the entire matter. Long after cultures, nations, states, tribes, governments and socio-political systems come and go, **spiritual life, spirituality, and religion** enduringly remain.

The active concern for relationships distinguishes Jesus from the conventional and/or traditional concerns of his contemporaries. He stands out as different in this regard. When he takes time to connect with mothers' and their children, some disciples consider the children a nuisance and, time/attention given to them, an irritating distraction. Mark (10), notes Christ's relationship with children:

> *Once when some people where bringing their children to Jesus to bless them, the disciples shooed them away, telling them not to bother him. But when Jesus saw what was happening he was very much displeased with his disciples and said to them, "Let the children come to me...Don't send them away! ...Then he took the children into his arms and placed his hands on their heads and he blessed them.*

When a private (males only) meal is unexpectedly and inconveniently interrupted by a woman of ("the world's oldest profession") who is seeking forgiveness, healing, and wholeness while others present (including some of his disciples), with their outstanding religious beliefs in hand, express remote detachment and even furious indignation (Matthew 26). Jesus sees things differently. The unusual situation becomes a precious moment to demonstrate his relational concern/engagement:

> Jesus now proceeded to Bethany, to the home of Simon the leper. While he was eating, a woman came in with a bottle of very expensive perfume, and poured it over his head. The disciples were indignant. "What a waste of good money," they said. Why, she could have sold it for a fortune and given it to the poor." Jesus knew what they were thinking, and said, "Why are you criticizing her? For she has done a good thing to me. You will always have the poor among you, but you won't always have me. She has poured this perfume on me to prepare my body for burial. She will always be remembered for this deed. As Luke notes in chapter 7, Christ speaks in the hearing of all saying, "Therefore her sins - and they are many − are forgiven...And then speaking specifically to

her, says "Your sins are forgiven."...Your faith
has saved you; go in peace.

Christ's encounter and conversation with this woman exemplifies the relational qualities of acceptance, affirmation, empathy, and encouragement. In response, the woman begins her new life as one of his most devoted disciples (male or female) to have ever lived. What stands out in these representative examples is Christ's unswerving laser-like focus on, and concern for, relationships (all types of relationships). The foundation for all his activities was (from beginning to end) his relational concern. For example, his mandate to "Love God with all that you are and your neighbor as yourself" is a relational imperative. Wherever one turns in the Gospel narratives (short-biographies) of Christ, relationship is the central theme.

Returning to the woman at the well, Jesus is concerned with the nature and quality of the relational experience. He begins with this in mind, she does not. Her point of engagement is quite different. In her statement "You are a Jewish man and I am a Samaritan woman," and in the ensuing exchange, (as we all are often inclined to do), she puts ethnic, tribal, gender, culture, custom, religion and doctrinal issues *first*, these are her chief concerns. Jesus does not go there with her.

Refusing to engage in *religious polemics* and without *disparaging, dismissing or invalidating* her religion, gender, ethnicity, and marital status, he is not distracted or diverted from his original intent to share his truth with her, by *first* entering into a relationship with her.

Instead, Jesus *transforms and transcends* the entanglements of conventionality, gender roles, longstanding ethnic grievances, intractable religious differences, disagreements, and divisions standing between them. His first concerned is to initiate and build upon a foundation for relationship that would enrich their mutual spiritual journey toward ever increasing spiritual comprehension, his own, hers, and (as the narrative goes on to reveal), her community as well). Whatever one thinks of Jesus, his character, message and mission, this entire encounter typifies his universal intention to enrich, improve and enhance the significant relationships that constitute life. The fundamental dynamic that draws people of the world to Christ is *a relationship of trust*. The justification of his claims is confirmed in his relational impact on the vital relationships that all people are concerned about.

While many of his purported followers (past and present) often wallow in self-excusing evasions, there is no ambiguity in Christ: a faith that fails to demonstratively honor and actively affirm *a relation-centered spirituality and is severed from actual relationships, is worthless and absolutely dispensable.*

His supreme *redemptive concern* is to enhance, enrich and improve these relationships. He expects and exhorts his disciples/followers (past, present, and future), to thoroughly embrace, promote, and faithfully follow his example. *Jesus puts relationships first.* And this is why I love Christ, serve him, and strive, by every means possible in this life, (enabled and empowered by his Spirit), to follow his lead (both near and far).

People within the GSC (as individuals and groups), just I've done, have a splendid opportunity, (even an obligation), to tell and show the world, how, and to what extent a focus on relationships (as set forth in these pages), typifies their own particular spiritual homes, faiths, endeavors, enterprises, missions, policies, programs, and practices.

When **relationships** don't matter, and are not prioritized, life is in jeopardy, people, (individually and collectively), in any given context, under any set of circumstances or situations, are wounded, broken, crushed, and oppressed. When, and where these conditions show up in the world (near or far), we must look for, and assess the responses from the GSC. What is its role, function and involvement, what does it do, is the GSC a preoccupied observer, a reluctant by-stander, or an active participant in the calamitous mix of mayhem, destruction, and death?

There is another a way to experience **spiritual life, spirituality, and religion,** it is qualitatively different, richer, in fact superior, and incomparably more truthful and life-affirming than **the pseudo- spiritual priorities** of hollow convention, sterile intellectualism, ecclesiastical domination, and group exclusiveness. Explore a relational understanding, comprehension, perspective, and approach to spiritual experience. Investigate and Consider *Relational Spirituality (R/S)*:

A **spiritual philosophy** that commits itself to comprehend, express, and communicate **spiritual life, spirituality and religion** in the **thought, language, and vocabulary of relationship.** Like the earth orbits the sun, everything of significance in life and spiritual experience revolves around **the centrality of relationship.**

CHAPTER SIX
Relational Spirituality (R/S): The Relational Priority

R/S involves the awareness, experience, expression, pursuit, (and, realistically), even the evasion of relationship with a Spiritual Referent and/or a Transcendent Spiritual Source, oneself, one's community, other communities, our planet, planets explored and the cosmos in which all are situated.

Experience confirms that there are two things in life that are uniquely yours, first, your **existence** and secondly, your unique **experience**, both occur in the realm of relationship in which a constellation of relationships shape, inform, influence, and ultimately determine (non-fatalistically), the quality (or lack thereof) of your life experience. This means, in effect, that life is the sum total of all the various relationships we will ever experience in our lifetime.

Our relationships are the real stories of our lives and they matter on a grand-scale. Life as the sum of our relationships, is axiomatic in R/S. Life is not a theoretical construct configured in analytical postulates, evidences, equations, propositions, and mechanistic systems. Life is supremely relational, the sum of which is measured in terms of our actual relationships (their quality or lack thereof).

Candidness and honesty (with self and others) about what we are actually experiencing in our relationships (not what we merely imagine, idealize, or hope for) is integral to R/S. Frontal encounters with the encouraging and/or disappointing relational realities from which we, in the long run, cannot hide, are essential and part of the bargain with life. In all types of relationships, (from people in the community, to the peoples of the world), the aim (in the context of our human relatedness), is the mutual and reciprocal improvement, enhancement and enrichment of the relationships we experience.

No matter how far afield one may go while navigating the challenging contours, and negotiating the inevitable twists and turns of life (in the journey through it), she/he will inevitably return to this simple, yet profound reality again and again, and again: life happens within the orbit of our relationships.

Responsive to this reality, *the relational experience* is both the point of *departure and final destination* in R/S. We do not say that R/S will produce a heaven on earth, eliminate all problems, troubles, distress, and discomforts. We also know, that in this life, we don't always get everything we want in our relationships, but what we do get, we must (as individuals and groups), contribute our part, ceaselessly working for that which we *do* want. We must not fear, duck, bob, and weave around the question, what is our part? Usually, in the long run, it is better not to flee from, but to run toward, our greatest relational fears.

R/S is not a giddy new trend, though it can bring on a stimulating buzz. It is not an *inspirational tract*, yet it inspires. It compels and motivates, but it isn't a *motivational piece.* It is very helpful and encouraging, but not a *self-help* guide for spiritual life. While R/S requires action, it is not *a program for religious activism.* It advocates and promotes spiritual development, yet it is not *a manual for spiritual growth*. More than these, R/S is a comprehensive *spiritual philosophy and frame of reference, a guide for spiritual life, an anchor and foundation for a practical realized spirituality.* After we turn out the lights on hollow speech, shun all qualifiers, cut out religious static, trim spiritual fat from religious convention and spiritual conformity, filter and distill spiritual experience into its primary essence, *R/S* is what we finally get down to.

R/S is not *anti-intellectual* (hostile to words, concepts, theories, and ideas). It simply and clearly recognizes that, standing alone, they calcify and impede spiritual experience. In isolation, they do not exemplify or authenticate spiritual profundity, power, and vitality.

All persons (family, friends, strangers, refugees etc.), experience themselves and their lives in the midst of *actual relationships* (not in the dry grass, weeds and stalks of cold statements and idea fests). Much is at stake here. There are various degrees of *relational* problems, conflicts, grievances, disputes, strife, difficulties, polarizations, and wars, that strain, brake, and wound relationships within, between, and among *all communities* (religious and secular), on the planet.

None is exempt. No one is immune. All, on a grand scale, are in need of help, health, and healing. There are no claims or promises of moral-ethical perfection in R/S. Human limitations are admittedly in play here, but then, so are human capabilities. There are many things we cannot do, just as there many things we can do. And most importantly, **extraordinary** things can happen when **spiritual power** (the key factor on which everything turns), operates in and through the relationships we engage, encounter, sustain, and, when necessary, conclude).

Relationally adverse, religious systems that suggest **spiritual maturity** by merely invoking or chanting **right words, right doctrines, right system recitations,** are powerless and ineffective in the lives of those who believe that in doing so, **right things** will follow, in the **absence of personal, social, and institutional transformations.**

We who comprehend, embrace, exemplify, and promote R/S, boldly assert, without reservation, free of ambiguity and equivocation, that:

> *Many things matter in spiritual life, spirituality, and religion: But, actual relationships (their quality or lack thereof), matter most, more than any other competing interest, consideration, and concern.*

R/S begins with relationships, not religious and/or theological apologetics (*non-relational,* promotional/rational/intellectual defenses of one's own faith/spiritual perspective). R/S does not qualify itself on the grounds of a paper in hand sacred text, a special place, tradition or custom. A spiritual entity, leader, sage, guru, or enthusiast, expecting (often demanding), *unearned authenticity, credibility, trust,* and *automatic allegiance,* solely on the basis of statements of belief (without demonstration), codified teaching (detached from experience), and practices (disengaged from life), is disqualified as a trustworthy and reliable source of spiritual truth. Truthfulness and integrity are painstakingly gained. And genuine confirmation is neither free, nor an entitlement. The acknowledgement of human frailty and fallibility in religion, as in all things, doesn't preclude principled guidelines and criteria that help us to be at our spiritual best. This requires standards. R/S adheres to, and counsels a standard of its own creation.

The Spiritual Optics Test (SOT)

The ordinary, usual, and traditional grounds and means *religions* employ to garner public trust, respect, and acceptance above, no longer (as was often the case in days of greater glory past), qualify as sufficient evidences of spiritual veracity today.

Now, spiritual legitimacy and authenticity stand or fall on *optics* (the simple eye test). Never again ought one believe, follow, let alone teach, that which cannot be ascertained or optically verified. When vying for public acceptance and allegiance, people of all faiths must reacquaint themselves with an old adage my beloved grandmother would often cite to point out some incongruities in my youthful behavior) "What you do speaks so loudly, that I cannot hear what you say."

Pass the SOT, and gain authenticity and credibility, fail it, and summarily forfeit both. There are only two possible outcomes in this test: *test in, or test out*.

No spiritual perspective, religion, faith, tradition, path, or movement is exempt or excused from this standard. Under the gaze of truth, honesty, and veracity none can evade the SOT for long. It will not fail to reveal spiritual fraudulence, manipulation, and pretension in all their colorful apparel, as well as the anchoring illuminations of truth, trust, and integrity.

The Sacred Self In Relational Spirituality

We contend that relationship with "oneself" impacts, and is linked to one's relationship with God, one's community, and other communities and with other-selves. In speaking of "self" and "soul," what do we have in mind? In terms of "the soul," Jung says: "...the self is our life's goal, for it is the completest expression of the fateful combination we call individuality..."

Curtis D. Smith, in his book *Jung's Quest for Wholeness* (1990:66) understands and speaks of the collective unconscious as contents that are "universal and timeless." In this sense (according to Jung) *the actuality of the essential self* is an original aspect of human existence and nature (an original reality) not acquired through subsequent experience as some suggest. Jung places "the self" at the apex of his psychological concern.

Hebraic thought in the Old Testament period beginning with Abraham (ca. 1921 B.C.E.) indicates that the embodied self (also soul or living being) is endowed with soul (nephesh), spirit (ruach) and heart (leb). They are not parsed, distinct, and perceived as mutually exclusive. Modern distinctions between self and soul, heart and mind (a Western perspective), are alien to the Hebraic conception of life. In Hebrew thought, self, soul, heart, and mind appear to be interchangeable and synonymous. To speak of one, is to simultaneously speak of the other. Equivalent in meaning, they are not understood as separate modes, and categories of existence, but indicate a living, undivided, unified psychological-spiritual and emotional being. The Greek near equivalent word (from a philosophical perspective) for the soul as life's "animating principle," (by transliteration) is "psuche," for the heart "kardia," and "nous" for the mind.

In R/S, the *self* is individualized, unique, personal and sacred. We are sacred selves because of our relatedness and connection (conscious and unconscious) to God. Our spiritual identity as spiritual beings is the ground of our sacredness. There is no sensible grammatical or compelling literary reason to isolate, divide, separate or make distinctions among the words self, soul and spirit. They are not separate, distinct or set apart from each other.

They are integrative/interchangeable words indicating a spiritually unified holistic identity, existence, and experience. This explains why we feel and think of our *individual selves* as one singular holistic spiritual being, not *three separate entities.*

Consequently, we are not contemptible wastrels. By virtue of simply being human (and not by fortune, fame or circumstance), all persons possess inherent value that defies statistical measurement and arbitrary social norms. We are on solid ground to take a high view of our intrinsic worth, value and significance.

We are not worthless or useless. Our individual lives have purpose and meaning. We are not sacred simply because we have been told so (though we should be told often), or because we happen to feel that we are (though such feeling is vital for us). Our sacredness (the sacred self) is not contingent upon our particular conditions, circumstances, or experiences.

What confirms and assures us of our sacredness is that it is anchored in, and emerges from our relatedness and connection to God. We can, and must categorically reject, confront, and counter all that would assault, negate and diminish this truth.

This view of the sacred self encourages, rather than exempts us from the quest for spiritual enlivenment or rebirth, a theme found (from earliest times) in the ideas and practices of most all religions, spiritual paths and movements. Each one, in diverse and multiple ways, concur with Christ's exhortation, that at some point in life, "You must experience a spiritual rebirth" (a spiritual enlivenment).

A religion or spiritual path may exhort adherents and followers to negate and resist self-serving self-interests by way of self-denial, but this form of *self-denial is not an exhortation to, and does not call for, or mandate the denial of the sacred self.* To marginalize or mute this truth is spiritual dereliction. In R/S, the *sacred self* is, without equivocation, a non-negotiable spiritual absolute to be acknowledged, celebrated and enjoyed.

Heschel, in *God in Search of Man: A Philosophy of Judaism* (1955: 396, 397) speaks to this individual dimension of the self from the angle of self-centeredness and the human tendency toward selfishness (as in the individual "promoting his own prosperity"...as in "a life dedicated to self-indulgence") to the detriment of others. He notes that:

> There is, indeed, a perpetual tension in man between the focus of the self and the goal that lies beyond the self. Animal life is a state of living driven by forces regardless of examined goals. Animal in man is the drive to concentrate on the satisfaction of needs; spiritual in man is the will to serve higher ends, and in serving ends he transcends his needs. To say that the yearning to be free of selfish interests is as selfish as any other interest is semantic confusion. The difference is in the intention or direction of the act. Selfish interests are centripetal; freedom from selfish interests is centrifugal, a turning away from the self. The essence of man, his uniqueness, is in his power to surpass the self, to rise above this needs and selfish motives. To ignore the seriousness of that tension is to live in a fool's paradise; to despair of the power to deal with it is to move into cynic's inferno.

But the polarity to the individual self is the self of another. Heschel addresses this relationship also, in his earlier book, *Man is not Alone: A Philosophy of Religion*. Attempting to connect and unite these polarities he offers the following:

> A man entirely unconcerned with his self is dead; a man exclusively concerned with his self is a beast...the child becomes human not by discovering the environment which includes things and other selves, but by becoming sensitive selves...At first the other selves are considered as means to attain the fulfillment of his own needs...as a result of various events, such as observing other peoples suffering, falling in love or by being morally educated, he begins to acknowledge others as ends, to respond to their needs even regardless of personal expediency...

He goes on to say:

> It is not true that man is condemned to life imprisonment in a realm of wherein causality, struggle for existence, will to power, libido, sex, and the craving for prestige are the only springs for action. He is involved in relations that run beyond their

realm. There is no man who does not strive, at one time or another, for some degree of disinterestedness; who does not seek something to which he could attach regardless of advantage. It is not true that all men are at all times at the mercy of their ego, that promoting their own prosperity is all they can do. It is not true that in the conflicts of honesty and expediency, the first is always defeated. In every soul there lives incognito, a coercion to love, to forget oneself, to be independent of vested interests...he often resists the tempting rewards of wealth, power, or vulgar popularity; that he foregoes the approval of favor of those who dominate the financial, political or academic world for the sake of remaining loyal to a moral or religious principle.

This individual dimension of the self, confronts us with matters, issues and processes of individual psycho-spiritual-emotional healing, growth and development toward greater wholeness in relation to one's own individual self. The process of becoming oneself more fully requires conscious intention and active participation. ***Self-knowledge and self-understanding are not acquired automatically.*** If not actively pursued they will not occur. Understanding the self in this manner helps one to develop the foundational thinking that supports the creative structures needed to put this view into practical action in one's own life. In addition, recognizing and honoring the sacred self helps one to shake off the shroud and disperse the fog of *self-ignorance that makes one a stranger to oneself and an enigma to others.*

Obstacles to the Self

One's psycho-spiritual-emotional growth as an *individual self* is contingent on a consciously active engagement in a healing work allowing us to move from a wounded fragmented self, toward a self that is progressively being healed and made more whole.

One obstacle encountered in this journey is the naïve and erroneous notion that anything to do with the self must always be framed in the negative. In Christian context, this happens (as may be recalled) when some erroneously understand and interpret Christ's statement (Lk. 9:23) regarding *"self-denial"* as an exhortation to *"deny the self."* These terms (as we earlier demonstrated) are not spiritual equivalents. Christ never denigrated or disparaged the Sacred Self. And nowhere does he condemn or discourage the progressive psycho-spiritual-emotional growth of human beings (his own included). Another obstacle one may meet along the path to spiritual self-development is the attempt to elude or become deaf to the call to *know oneself*, to move from infantile self-ignorance to a maturing self-knowledge. Jung has termed this call a *"summons to the self."* This call reaches its highest pitch and intensity at a critical period in life, usually the last half of our lives (ordinarily at 45 and beyond). Though many hear it, only some consciously and actively respond, and they grow forward. Should one feel/hear it, then take stock, and heed it.

This point in one's life was, according to Jung, for *"...the development of a dialog with the Self,"* something we may have given scant attention to because of other *pre-occupations* earlier in life.

An additional obstacle to the self is the flat-out refusal and/or simple ignorance of looking within ourselves as the pre-condition/core aspect of our potential spiritual growth. *The real journey to oneself begins with and within oneself*. This requires engaging in processes of self-knowledge that we may come to clearer and truer understandings of how we became who we find ourselves to be, and continue to become.

Most people (religious and secular) want to experience abundant life (psycho-spiritually-emotionally and physically). Progressively knowing oneself is key factor for abundant living. Knowledge (as in experiencing) God's Presence and knowledge (as in experiencing) oneself, is not an either/or proposition. Rather than being antithetical, they are complimentary. Where is the spiritual value in knowing God, if such knowledge discourages and excludes knowing oneself? What spiritual value is there in knowing oneself, if such knowledge denigrates and dismisses knowing God who is the source of one's life?

Understanding the absolute necessity of self-growth for a fuller, deeper and richer life, Plotinus said "look within" and the Delphic Council, urges, "know thyself." The most significant growth in our lives is not brought about by a constant preoccupation with all that is outside of ourselves (the outward gaze), it always begins in just one way; by going within and starting with oneself.

R/S affirms and encourages constructive self-reflective processes as essential psycho-spiritual tools for self-discovery and a richer life. Engaging in this developmental process we become better known to ourselves and to many others in our lives.

We have seen that most members of GSC, on some level, acknowledge the self as sacred. Most everyone senses (individually and collectively) their worth and value. We resist diminishment and devaluation of who we are. We naturally recoil, and seek to protect ourselves from assault upon our sacred selves. At every point, R/S recognizes and acknowledges the *Sacred Self.*

The Divine Presence

Speaking of the Divine Presence as an intellectual exercise is disastrously substandard and unproductive. Those who do so demonstrate an extremely narrow spiritual acumen that must be challenged to find its way into deeper depth and fuller expansion. This thin approach is religiously unreliable and spiritually deficient. In depth and detail, this limited approach is a severe spiritual impediment. A better and more trustworthy approach is that which involves, as we recall, the whole person (heart, mind, body and soul). Most religiously inclined and spiritually engaged persons and groups in the GSC acknowledge (in different languages and by differing names) God, or generically, a "Divine Presence" as the Source of all life and creation.

Some perceive this "presence" as an impersonal cosmic principle/power, which is the source of all and from which everything, and everyone has emerged. For others, the Divine Presence is simply the universe or nature itself. And there are yet others, (agnostics, atheist, skeptics, etc.) for whom the very notion of a Divine Presence is not at all a settled matter.

A broad range of feelings, thoughts, perceptions and experiences orbit the matter of a divine presence (we will present some of these). Responses to the notion of a divine presence range rather widely, from reverence to revulsion, approach or avoidance, love to fear, bliss to blistering, guilt to grace and gratitude, belief to disbelief and doubt, ambivalence to indifference, disdain to distortion and illusion, dislocation to anger and alienation. In some fundamental, practical and perhaps mystical and mysterious way, most everyone responds and reacts to the matter or question of a "Divine Presence." Many feelings and thoughts come to mind when speaking of a "Divine Presence." The faithful of all traditions/paths proclaim and passionately defend the notion. It is perennially debated, vigorously disputed and totally rejected by others. And coalitions of the wise and multitudes of the foolish, found in all walks of life, are often clueless on the subject.

Adherents and followers of most faiths want to see, hear, listen and respond to who, or what they perceive as God or "Divine Presence." Some ask, is this presence knowable? And what does such knowledge mean and entail? Is it about an experience, a feeling, a sensing, a faith, or a simple belief, or all of the above?

Quite often it is in relation to a "Divine Presence" that sacred texts emerge, religious claims are made, creeds of faith are constructed, forms of worship are established and converts are made (and lost).

In Hinduism for example, the "Divine Presence" and essence (according to the Vedas/Upanishads) is **Brahman,** of which **all** are expressions. On this basis (as in

New Thought) *the self is considered divine.* In Judaism the "Divine Presence" (according to the Pentateuch/Torah/Talmud) is **Yahweh or Jehovah.** That presence in Christianity (according to the Old and New Testaments) is God as (Father, Son and Holy Spirit). In Islam that presence (according to the Qur'an) is **Allah.**

By way of comparison, basic tenants of the International Metaphysical Ministry (I.M.M.) clearly indicate that the Divine Presence dwells and is found in all of life, specifically that:

> There ultimately is but one life in this universe, God the Creator individualized and seeking expression through all creation...The Universal Life Presence of God exists in all living things, as the creating and life sustaining force within its creation...And that, the point of contact with the Presence of God is at the center of the human mind. This can be experienced spontaneously in meditation or by other means and practices.

Like I.M.M., many other New Thought expressions of religious faith and spiritual life, establish their views regarding the "Divine Presence" (and other cardinal beliefs) on an allegorical/symbolic interpretation and understanding of the Christian Bible in conjunction with valuable insights found in the sacred texts (and philosophical ideas) of other world religions, traditions and movements.

Comparatively speaking, all of the many aforementioned apprehensions of the "Divine Presence" attempt to say something about this reality often from differing angles (more precisely) experiences. While maintaining certain distinctions, each exhibits some qualities and interests of the other, demonstrating a creative connecting link between religious particularity and spiritual universality.

Also, in the matter of the Divine Presence, people naturally have questions for and about God. Feeling and thoughts toward God, the "Divine Presence," range from love and reverence, consolation and comfort, guilt and shame, connection and disconnection, wholeness and fragmentation, grace and gratitude, joy and peace, approach and avoidance, ignorance and indifference, to trust, doubt, fear, and anger.

R/S explores such questions as, if Divine love and compassion exist why is the world filled with sickness, suffering, evil and injustice? Why are we victims of immoral devastating wars, natural disasters, cataclysmic social upheavals, debilitating illnesses, and finally death, the grim reaper? If God is caring, kind and just, why isn't there more joy, beauty, peace, happiness and fulfillment? If there is a "Divine Presence" why are we subject to, and not shielded from, the vexations in life that scar, break and crush us and those we love? Who and where is the "Divine Presence" in the face of these merciless boots on the ground experiences? And what does God's presence or absence to, and for humanity?

Is this "Presence" plausible or moreover, even detectible? If there is a "Presence" is that presence anything more than a transcendental X? These are frontline, cutting edge questions people from all walks of life are searchingly asking, according to the light they have. No single response can satisfy all such concerns. And every spiritual response is shaped by various postures of understanding, faith and belief.

What makes the matter of God, the Divine Presence, of greatest importance to us is its polarity, the absence of God. The whole world turns differently depending on where one stands in relation to these two, very real, polarities. Experiencing God, the "Divine Presence" within and about us, strengthens our faith, deepens our comfort, heightens our confidence, and empowers our own *presence* in the world *R/S operates on the basis of a faith that assures us that God is relational and always present with us.*

The "Beloved Community"

Nothing exemplifies our need for connection and a place of belonging quite like community. We fear and recoil from the prospects of an isolated lonely life. We want a communal experience that extends beyond individual selves and embraces others. Something very deep within us compels us to experience life in community. Is a "beloved community" a romanticized, utopian notion?

Not so, for Dr. M.L. King. He envisioned an actualized community to our consciousness. Though marches, sit-in, boycotts, jail-ins, and other strategic tactics were employed in the American struggle waged by African-Americans and their allies, to achieve their constitutional and civil rights, he reminded people what the goal of the movement was "The end is reconciliation, the end is redemption, the end is the creation of the beloved community" King challenged us (individually and collectively, on any level possible), to participate in its realization. Authentic connection, belonging, bonding and creative self-less service are hallmarks of a "beloved community."

Such a community desires and actively pursues a relational life, to experience life in relation to, and with others. Individuals and groups thrive and prosper. Hearts are open and everyone is honored, valued, affirmed, and safe. Masks, disguises, and pretentions are bid farewell. People share and hold in common their cares, concerns, comforts, joys, accomplishments, hopes, and dreams, as well as their difficulties, flaws, flops, and failures without fear of judgment, reprisal, recrimination, shame, shunning, dishonor, or banishment. They bond together as traveling companions, pioneers, explorers, seekers, settlers, and creative builders. A "beloved community" is not a conflict-free zone, or effortlessly realized. It is not established and sustain by sincerity alone. Rooted in love, a "beloved community" is created and established by the sustained engagement of its heart, soul, mind, values, intention, and will.

Life in a "beloved community" is not a denial of, or an escape from the imperfection and shortcomings, of our individual and collective selves. These realities do not lead this community to resignation or despair. Community is not an impossible quest for a new Eden. What Jung said about life is applicable to our beloved communities, *"To round itself out, life calls not for perfection but completion."*

Authentic life in community accepts and embraces everyone's being and existence. And finally, a "beloved community" challenges, compels, and helps all persons to actively participate in a way of life together, in which no one is dispensable and all are needed to experience its realization. From the vantage point of R/S, *A "beloved community" is a relational constellation in the realm of relationship.*

CHAPTER SEVEN
Relational Spirituality (R/S): The Indispensable Relational Qualities

Relational Spirituality is predicated on several indispensable relational qualities. Exemplified in conduct, these qualities are superior to lofty notions, laudable sentiments and good intentions. They are the seed from which principles, virtues, values and ideals come to life. These essential qualities are dispositional (reflecting a person's inner spiritual character and attitude). Internally compelled from within, they shape, determine and direct the world of one's daily relationships.

While not exhaustive, these qualities powerfully energize, improve, enhance and enrich who we are and whom we are with. Each is a life force. Collectively, they are capable of healing and transforming our relationships as well as transcending what engulfs us. It would be a misunderstanding of these relational qualities if they were viewed as a panacea.

The complexity of who we are as persons will always require the inclusion and integration of all that is available to us from many quarters for our psycho-spiritual-emotional-physical wellbeing. Yet, individuals and communities can accomplish more in a single day, exhibiting these qualities, than is possible in a lifetime without them.

It must also be recognized that theses relational qualities will be challenged and opposed by the daily mechanisms of human self-serving, self-interests that everyone and all groups are demonstrably capable of.

Rogers M. Smith sets forth the inevitable and perennial conflict between the best ideals, virtues and qualities of American civic life and the fact of their inegalitarian applicability to all Americans. Of his own experience (1997:3) he writes:

> I then grew up in Springfield, Illinois, the adult home of Abraham Lincoln. In those years, the civil rights movement spurred bitter antagonism in the South that I frequently visited. Hence painful arguments about the proper racial and religious character of America were a vivid part of my youth. I also knew well that sincere if horribly wrong beliefs in racial and gender inequality and Protestant superiority were common not

only among my genteel Southern relatives but also among the pillars of my Northern church and community. Many good people defended inegalitarian principles of social ordering far more stubbornly than any doctrines of universal human rights or republican government. Probably because of this background, the evidence of American citizenship laws soon led me to conclude, against much of my education, that the intellectual and political traditions conceiving of America in an inegalitarian racial, patriarchal and religious terms had long been as much a part of American life as the liberal and republican doctrines that scholars stressed.

Other examples show that vital ideals, virtues and qualities can be relationally realized. In tribute to Gandhi's example of living out the relational quality of love in his effort to demonstrate a nonviolent approach to India's independence from imperial Britain, Martin Luther King Jr., in *A Testament of Hope: The Essential Writings of Martin Luther King, Jr.* (1992:38) said:

As I delved deeply into the philosophy of Gandhi my skepticism concerning the power of love gradually diminished, and I came to see for the first time that the nonviolence was one of the most potent weapons available to oppressed people in their struggle for freedom...consciously or unconsciously I was driven back to the Sermon on the Mount and the Gandhian method of nonviolent resistance. Christ furnished the spirit and motivation while Gandhi furnished the method.

King received the Nobel Peace Prize in 1964.

R/S demonstrates, promotes, and advocates specific relational qualities that are indispensable. They do not exhaust the lexicon of relational qualities. Yet, when embraced, they nurture and sustain quality relationships across the entire spectrum of the lives we live. In their absence, we do not experience the quality relationships we need, desire, deserve and long for.

Acceptance

Acceptance is paramount. We can never come to genuinely know and fully love another person until we have first accepted that individual. Relationships are far less than what they could be, until acceptance, (held in common and shared together) is operative. Full cylindered, acceptance never lacks mutuality and reciprocity. Acceptance is always the first and continuing attitude towards oneself and all persons we come into relationship with.

Acceptance means that we naturally accept the individuality, uniqueness, value and worth of another without attaching or requiring subjective and/or arbitrary preconditions. Persons are accepted as they are, not as one might wish or insist them to be. We are accepted in the Divine, and we accept the Divine in ourselves and in all others. Where there is authentic love, there is genuine acceptance. Acceptance and all of the ensuing qualities can be summed up in a single grand thought; God, the Divine Presence accepts us, we accept ourselves and one another.

Affirmation

When acceptance of oneself and all others is free of, and followed by, the openhearted affirmation of oneself and others, relationships soar. One can (and does) choose to affirm or negate in relation to self and others. These two possibilities stand in stark contrast. Negation is oppressive. Affirmation is a breath of fresh air and a wonderful ray of light. Negation punctures hope, saps vitality, burdens the heart and weighs down the soul. The quality of affirmation can and must also find its way into daily speech, affecting daily experiences, conditions and circumstances.

Dr. Paul L. Masters (International Metaphysical Ministry, University of Metaphysics and the University of Sedona) puts great emphasis on the constructive power and force of affirmational statements in spiritual life. He notes that:

> "to treat the negative condition of the 'mind' by nullifying and replacing it with an 'affirmation for spiritual sublimation.' For example, when confronted with 'worry-doubt' one is advised to affirm 'I entrust my life and circumstances to the Power of the GOD-MIND within me, and I accept that all is made well already.' Or, in the case of 'jealousy-envy' one is counseled to affirm 'I accept that the HIGHER GOD-MIND already knows my needs and without taking from anyone has ALREADY supplied me, as of now.'"

In R/S, affirmation instills confidence, comfort and hope throughout one's being, becoming our constant positive companion. The enduring richness and beauty of affirmation lies in the fact that it always uplifts us.

Cultivating a predisposition to affirm others/self is especially significant and absolutely necessary for communities and cultures plagued by spirits of pervasive negativism and climates of destructive judgment. God, the Divine Presence, affirms us and we affirm ourselves and one another.

Support

We need and must have one another's daily support. The spirit, disposition, and attitude of support are at their best (as are the other accompanying relational qualities) when support is mutual and reciprocal. For its richest impact, we need to experience support in many forms (psycho-spiritual-emotional-physical). We need to have another person and/or a community's supportive spirit and active presence when we're buckled over by life's inescapable challenges. Deep within ourselves we prosper and bloom when someone or some community supports us in our projects, endeavors and dreams. If no one supports us, we trudge through the bleakness. Unsupported, the ground beneath our feet is taken away. We're shaken, often fearful, feeling completely alone and abandoned. Support assures us that we are never in it alone. God, the Divine Presence supports us and we support ourselves and one another.

Encouragement

What is a more comforting, revitalizing and strengthening quality in relationships nourished by love, than encouragement? Encouragement is important to us because the challenges of life are deep, high and wide. Everyone meets discouragement in the journey of life. Unrelieved, it drains and can deplete our psycho-spiritual-emotional resources. Unyielding, discouragement can bring us to the gates of exhaustion and collapse. Adverse health, medical and financial matters can disturb and trouble us. We encounter a cascade of joy and pain, hope and despair, happiness and sadness.

We experience real triumphs and apparent defeats. There are also risks, sacrifices, doubts, fears, and uncertainties along the way. This is when a word of cheer, a kindly presence lending strengthening care and action heartens us. Through encouragement, one moves from hopelessness and distress into peace, confidence and stability. We are renewed. Our feelings and sense of meaning, purpose and worth are restored. In an economy of words, God, the Divine Presence encourages us and we encourage ourselves and one another.

Empathy

When we are transparent about our concerns, difficulties, struggles, trials, calamities, fears, and hopes with someone or others, what is possible? Our experience (thus our very self) could be invalidated. We could also encounter emotional distancing, indifference and criticism. This hits us hard. We take it personally, as we surely will, because it is indeed, an extremely personal situation. We fear and recoil from cold indifference and the void of emotional distance. We are drawn to compassionate and empathetic understanding of our concerns. The warmth of empathy validates and attracts us. Its absence repels us. Listening tempered with empathy consoles and bolsters us. Empathy is free of criticism and faultfinding. Our relationships are characterized by empathy as we open-heartedly share in, bear with, and uphold one another in the midst of any trouble, any need and any concern. God, the Divine Presence empathizes with us and we empathize with one another.

Service

We tilt toward, and tend to live our lives preoccupied with our own issues, considerations and concerns. But we can awake to a service-consciousness that is self-transcendent. We actualize the relational quality of service when our presence, actions, involvement and participation in the lives of others finds exhibition through demonstration. This may involve service in a cause, a calling, a mission, an endeavor or enterprise. Service involves being beneficially useful in some capacity that moves us beyond the self-enclosed circles of our own lives. The quality of service yokes us with someone and/or others to accomplish, realize and bring to fruition vital practical needs, dreams and visions through constructive self-expenditure. Gratitude often compels us to service.

A spirit of service often emerges within us as an expression of gratitude in response to what someone/or others, have done on our behalf, perhaps in response to having been rescued in some significantly unforgettable way. Service can be and is often our individualized offering in recognition of the love, light and grace we have received through the passionate service of others who opened their hearts to us. In following their examples, we reciprocate. The relational quality of service is firmly anchored in the certainty that everyone has something to give that others need for their psycho-spiritual-emotional-physical health and wellbeing (time, abilities, materials, gifts, talents, insights, perspectives, et.) So then, we serve God, the Divine Presence and in doing so, we serve one another.

Unity

Genuine unity (if it authentically exists at all) is what we concretely have as an antidote to the voluminous, never ending talk about it. Other common blocks and impediments to unity are a twisted sense of pride, the vulgarity of arrogance, demented self-righteousness, ruthless ambition and shameless greed. Unfortunately, the fact is, there are people from all walks of life who actively oppose the spirit and actualization of unity. Where an authentic spiritual unity does exist, those opposed to it seek its demise. Consequently, unity must be courageously defended. The fires of disunity must be extinguished for unity's maintenance.

The relational quality of unity is a unity of spirit, thought, feeling and action in relation to what is deemed of greatest significance and of most importance regarding the quality of our relationships. In essence, God, the Divine Presence is "One" in unity, and we are one in unity with one another.

Peace

Authentic peace cannot be imposed. Peace is not present because hostilities are kept at bay. Peace is present where hostilities (inward and outward) no longer exist. Relational peace is genuine as hostilities are replaced by mutual and reciprocal exchanges of trust, confidence, respect, understanding and goodwill. Peace is not disturbance or conflict-free. It too, has its perennial foes (grievances, anger, fear, hatred, envy, jealousy, arrogance, avarice, revenge and the like). In R/S peace involves the disposition of one's spirit. Peace is an inner orientation. Bearers of peace have hearts of peace and peace of mind. They are a soul-force for peace. As we are disposed to peace, it is within our ability and power to create and sustain it. Peace that originates within, will always find its life in the real world of our relationships. We may confidently affirm that we have peace with God and experience peace among ourselves.

Power

In times when much of life is being "de-spiritualized" we need, all the more, insight into spiritual power. The presence and expressions of power (or its lack thereof) are always with us. Power involves more than the mere ability to do something. In addition to having authority and the ability to get things done, power also involves our efforts to regulate, control, determine, direct, impose, shape, and govern our relationships with one another. Understanding power and identifying its sources, use, and purposes rightfully concerns us. Power can create or destroy, liberate or oppress, protect or plunder, foment evil or promote good. We quickly recognize visible powers (government, law, armed forces, economics, wealth, politics, science, technology and nature). These powers garner our immediate attention.

In R/S we looked beyond the immediate and apparent expressions of power, taking into account and emphasizing the power of the unseen; the invisible power (so to speak), of God, the Divine Presence.

In R/S, whatever powers that exist (visible, invisible, virtuous or vile), the decisive power is Divine Power. We affirm that the power of God, the Divine Presence is at work in our lives always and forever.

Truth

Is it true or false, a truth or a lie? Even if we should want to, we cannot, in the long run evade these questions. A falsehood can rise out of ignorance, a lie emerges from the intent to say or do something misleading, deceiving and contrary to truth. Lies disturb, distort and destroy relationships.

Relationships nourished and sustained by truth, rooted in love, give birth to fidelity and trust. We trust those who genuinely love us and entrust ourselves into their care. We seek, consider, and respect their advice and counsel. We do not fear that they will harm us, because they have not harmed us. We are vulnerable and open to their presence and involvement in our lives. We feel safe with them because we are safe with them. Untruth and falsehood subvert and assault our relationships. They are mortal enemies to truth and truthfulness. Truth is the Universe's guardian and protector. R/S embraces the relational quality of truth, affirming that God, the Divine Presence is as much TRUTH as is love, and truth is indispensable in the healing of our wounds and the liberation from what holds us captive.

Justice

Justice is a local and global matter that always engages us in the arena of relationships. What is made unjust must be re-made just. As a relational quality justice has many faces (psycho-spiritual-emotional-physical, socio-political-cultural-economic-law, etc.). Justice comes home to us most forcefully when it is denied us or when we are deprived of it through numerous injustices.

Experiencing the piercing sting and crushing bite of injustice first-hand dissolves our sometimes complacency and transforms us into staunch proponents and defenders of justice for all.

Dr. King reminded the world that "injustice anywhere is a threat to justice everywhere." Justice has meaning and integrity as we actualize it where injustices are found and unjust relationships exist. Everyone, and most certainly the wealthy, powerful and materially prosperous who own, operate and influence society's essential functions and quality of life, must vigilantly practice and enact justice equitably. As the prophet Amos wrote, we all must "Let justice roll on like a mighty river and integrity like a never failing stream."

Authentic justice is never self-serving (just for self). Societies suffer where justice is manipulated by and for a select elite while denied to all others. Wherever truth is sacred, justice triumphs, peace prevails and all people are safe, joyful and happy. Because life is essentially a spiritual experience, unjust relational attitudes and behaviors must become just through the transforming power of God, the Divine Presence, shaping, informing and guiding every other means available. The religiously inclined and spiritually engaged can advocate, practice, and promote just social transformations throughout the entire make-up of society from a variety of spiritual perspectives. The essence of the relational quality of justice can be summed up in one thought; Justice is of God, the Divine Presence, for all people everywhere, all the time.

In summation, the *relational qualities of R/S* are as follows:

> The acceptance, affirmation, support, and encouragement of all persons.

> Demonstrating and extending empathy (kindness and compassion) to everyone.

> Urging all persons to serve God and one another.

> The pursuit of unity and the securing of peace.

> The acknowledgement and demonstration of spiritual power.

> Active commitment to truth and justice (for and by) all persons.

CHAPTER EIGHT
Relational Spirituality (R/S): The 4 T's: Transition, Transformation, Transcendence, and Triumph

Comparative religion underscores the experience of spiritual sequence, that is to say, progression, expressed in differing ways, words, and practices that are peculiar and specific to each religion. **Buddhists** speak of the four "noble truths" and the "eightfold path." Hinduism speaks of fourfold aim (dharma/righteousness, artha/prosperity, kama/pleasure, and moksha/liberation) relative to the cycle of reincarnation. **Islam** stresses the "five pillars" of life, observance of dietary laws and "Jihad" variously understood. **Confucianism** points to tao/the way, te/virtue, jen/benevolence, and yi/courage, to do the right.

While interpretations and understandings vary, **Judaism and Christianity**, emphasize the sequence of creation, revelation temptation, fall, redemption and restoration as integral to the spiritual journey.

One can see the principle of spiritual progression in R/S as well. That sequence (as will be shown), begins with

transition followed by **transformation**, which leads into **transcendence** and culminates in **triumph, *the essential 4 T's of R/S.***

W. E. Vine's, *A Comprehensive Dictionary of the Original Greek Words with their Precise Meanings for English Readers* is a useful source book in understanding the meaning of these four words in the original Greek. Other languages will no doubt, have other words to express similar realities.

EPISTROPHE (meaning transition) is akin to the English word (conversion), implying a "turning about, or around, a turning from, and turning to." ***METAMORPHOO (meaning transformation)*** is akin to the English word (change), implying "a complete change which, under the power of God, will find expression in character and conduct." ***ANO*** (meaning transcendence) is akin to the English word (above), implying attunement to "a higher place," or pursuing "the things above," in contrast to that which is below/earthly. ***MIKAO*** (meaning triumph) is akin to the English word (conquer), synonymous with the English words "overcome", "victory", and "prevail", in contrast to "resignation" and "defeat."

In R/S, *Transition* is a spiritual change (instantaneously or progressive) from one spiritual condition/state to another. *Transformation* is spiritual change (radically instantaneously or gradual and progressive) from that which is negative and weak to that which is positive and strong. *Transcendence* is a constant spiritual disposition and behavior that rises above situations, conditions and energies that harm, wound and destroy − by creating and displacing them with what is spiritually healing, healthy and harmonious. *Triumph* is spiritual victory (instantaneous and/or progressive) over internal and external difficulties, obstacles, challenges, blocks and impediments to vital spiritual growth and development. It would be a mistake to understand these four words and what they signify, in terms of a magical/fail-safe spiritual formula or mechanical/clock-work religious method. Rather, they are to be understood in terms of a spiritual dynamic that is constant, continuous and sequential engaging the whole person and the whole of one's life.

The Specter of Self-Seeking, Self-Serving, Self-Interest

Within this spiritual sequence stands the *self's shadow and proclivity* to engage in, and be preoccupied with one's own selfish, self-serving, self-interest. Self-interest is not always pejorative. Self-interest is innate, necessary, constructive, and positive. However, when self-interest morphs into self-serving-self-interest it becomes a raging unquenchable tyrant capable of mass psycho-spiritual-moral-ethical injury and incalculable cultural and socio-political harm. From the relational perspective, selfish, self-serving-self-interest *decimates all types of relationships.*

As has been noted, without denying self, most religiously inclined and spiritually engaged persons/groups (the GSC for example), know that in spiritual life, there is a place for *self-denial (vigilance in the work of transcending self-serving-self-interest tendencies found in all people and common in every religion) for genuine spiritual development and authentic spiritual integrity.* Like it or not, the ever-present reality of self-serving-self-interest is with and within everyone, it is not an illusion. One is not, however, powerless in relation to this most powerful of human tendencies.

While self-serving-self-interest cannot be eradicated, it can (even within our human imperfections/limitations) be restrained, ameliorated, and to an effective degree, become less decisive in our lives. Individuals and groups can gain some degree of mastery over self-seeking, self-serving, self-interest (with Divine help), if one continuously counters it by/through the experiential spiritual sequence of **transition, transformation, transcendence and triumph presented here.**

CHAPTER NINE
The 4T's: What They Look Like in an Actual Life

In my own faith, a phenomenal example, of the 4 T's, (in my mind, the most dramatic in the New Testament), is exhibited in the life of that Hebrew follower of Christ, Saul of Tarsus, known by the English name Paul. Each of the 4 T's is vividly seen in what he particularly says of himself in the third chapter of Philippians. The first thing to notice is how he describes himself. He is a member of a specific ethnic group and heritage, his people, are the people of Israel. He was ritually circumcised (as was customary for male infants eight days after birth). He speaks of his tribal affiliation (a Benjamite). He says he was a "Hebrew of Hebrew," intimating that he was all Hebrew, Hebrew all the way. He cites his religious standing in his community as a Pharisee (a teacher of its religious laws and traditions).

He points to his zealous attacks upon those of another faith (the Christ ones). He adhered to the laws of his religious community to the degree that he was above reproach regarding them. In just a few paragraphs, he presents his ethnic, tribal, religious identity, zeal for his beliefs, his social standing and educational achievements, and of course his group affiliation (all the major components that constitute the *identity* that nurtured and sustained him). And then, shockingly, there is that explosive three letter word "But." After all he said about himself, expressing all the things that most people hold dear and are willing to die for, he now says, "I give them up and let them go. That which has enriched and elevated me in countless ways, I relinquish, and now count as *loss*." This astounding change is attributed to the 4 T's.

Having come to Christ, he *transitioned* from what he formerly was, and all he once prized and prioritized, because to know his Lord, mattered more than any other competing interest, consideration, and concern. He became *transformed* in character, disposition, vision, values, and purpose. He *transcended* *(and put into proper perspective and better use), h*is *prior* parochialisms of ethnicity, tribe, religion, and the props of social status, so that he could be and become that which Christ intended of him. In so doing, he *triumphed* over his former ways, patterns, inclinations, and proclivities. And in verse 17, he urged all within his reach, (which by extension includes contemporary followers of Christ) to follow his example. I encourage adherents of other religions, faiths, and traditions to share stories and examples of a similar nature, in a spirit of reciprocity and mutuality.

"Group Spirituality": The Group Priority

It is a fact, Glazer reminds us, that the "Peoples of America" consists of many ethnically self-conscious groups:

> Since the end of European mass immigration to this country...we have waited for the subsidence of ethnic self-consciousness, and often announced it, and it has returned again and again. But each time it has returned in so different a form that one could well argue it was not the same thing...what we saw was not the breakthrough of the consciousness of common origin and community that made America, but rather that ethnicity was...a more significant force.

Cruse also recognized the phenomenon of group identification in American life, pointing out that Americans live in a society whose:

> ...legal Constitution recognizes the rights, privileges, and aspirations of the individual, but whose political institutions recognize the reality of ethnic groups...that America, which idealizes the rights of the individual above everything else, is in reality, a nation dominated by the social power of groups, classes, in-groups and cliques – both ethnic and religious. The individual in America has few rights that are not backed up by the political, economic, and social power of one group or another...each individual American is a member of a group.

If Cruse and Glazer (both ethnic Americans, African and Jewish respectively) are right, the drive to make spiritual life, spirituality, and religion subservient to the self-seeking, self-serving interests is a dynamic component of group identification and affiliation.

Representative Voices In Religion

To stop here, we would exclude other vital religious voices, something the major (well known) religions are quite adept at. But people feel and think in different ways about religion. The historical and contemporary alliances and associations of the Metaphysical and New Thought communities come to mind. Their emphasis on the positive statement and practical demonstration of spiritual experience reaches and affirms many religiously inclined and spiritually engaged people in ways traditional faiths have been unable to do.

Some of their luminaries include, Joel S. Goldsmith, Charles, Myrtle and Lowell Fillmore, Eric Butterworth, Emmet Fox and Meister Eckhart of Germany. Goldsmith asked, "...how much of what we have read of spiritual revelation have we actually experienced? Lowell Fillmore said that, "the Kingdom of God is a spiritual state...when you abide in the Kingdom...you look out into the material world with a new spiritual vision...that pervades everything." Butterworth wrote, "Religion seems to have begun with an experience of transcendent oneness with the infinite. All the Scriptures of the world deal with the same theme: the description of that experience..."On ways in which religion and healing converge Fox wrote:

> Healing is only the beginning. When you are completely healed of everything wrong in your life – your body, your business, difficulties in personal relationships, obvious faults in your own character – you will not have finished your work. Your real work will only be commencing. Your real work is to show and experience the glory of God, to build the spiritual consciousness, "the house magnifical." This not to say that healing is unimportant – it has to precede the building.

The Christian metaphysician, theologian, and mystic Meister Eckhart of Germany addresses the religious intersection of contemplative prayer and engagement in life, noting that:

> The most powerful prayer, one well-nigh omnipotent, and the worthiest work of all is the outcome of the quiet mind. The quieter the mind, the more powerful, the worthier, the deeper, the more telling and more perfect the prayer is...Such a one can

do no deed, however small, that is not clothed with something of God's power and authority...pray that all our mortal members with their powers – eyes, heart, mouth, and all their senses – are turned in that direction...never stop until we find ourselves on the point of union with him we have in mind and are praying to, namely God.

Without dispensing with or negating the scientific orientation/method, Heschel, in, *God in Search of Man: A Philosophy of Judaism* addresses the "search for a voice of God in the world of man, in the following manner:

What are the grounds for certainty of the realness of God? It is clear that we cannot submit religion to scientific logic. Science is not the only way to truth, and its methods do not represent all of human thinking...they are out of place in that dimension of human existence in which God is the burning issue. God is not a scientific problem, and scientific methods are not capable of solving it. The reason why scientific methods are often thought to be capable of solving it is the success of their application in positive sciences. The fallacy involved in this analogy is that of treating God as if he were a phenomenon within the order of nature. The truth, however, is that

> the problem of God is not only related to phenomena within nature but to nature itself; not only to concepts within thinking but also to thinking itself.

Western dictionaries and encyclopedias provide numerous definitions of religion. The Penguin Dictionary of Religion defines religion as "A general term used...to designate all concepts concerning the beliefs in god (s) and goddess (es) as well as other spiritual beings or transcendental ultimate concerns. The American Heritage Dictionary in its turn, defines religion as a "belief in and reverence for supernatural power or powers regarded as creator and governor of the universe, and as a "personal or institutionalized system grounded in such belief and worship." In Merriam-Webster's Collegiate Dictionary we find that religion is said to be "a personal set or institutionalized system of religious attitudes, beliefs, and practices...a cause, principle." The Britannica Concise Encyclopedia (the only dictionary in this group to speak of religion as *relational*) defines it as a "Relation of human beings to God or the gods or to whatever they consider sacred or, in some cases, merely supernatural." In any event, (regardless of the languages employed) all such definitions are merely "statements." Statements of course, have an important place in spiritual awareness, expression and pursuit, but spiritual experience is paramount. Our actual experiences shape, color and inform our thoughts and feelings about spirituality.

Alongside these representative western definitions of religion stand representative western voices on religion. William James, more succinctly, stated that religion involves and engages people "as they apprehend themselves to stand in relation to whatever they consider divine." In his classic, *The World's Religions,* Huston Smith, an icon in the field of comparative religion, writes that "religion is...a way of life woven around a people's ultimate concerns...as a concern to align humanity with the transcendental ground of its existence." Demonstrating religion's universality and global similarities Huston adds:

> It is possible to climb life's mountain from any side, but when the top is reached the trails converge. At base, in the foothills of theology, ritual, and organizational structure, the religions are distinct.

147

Differences in culture, history geography, and collective temperament all make for diverse starting points...but beyond these differences, the same goal beckons.

More recently, with a greater feeling and alarming concern, he states in his book, *Why Religion Matters: The Fate of the Human Spirit in an Age of Disbelief,* that:

> The crisis that the world finds itself in as it swings on the hinge of a new millennium is located in something deeper than particular ways of organizing political systems and economies. In different ways, the East and the West are going through a single common crisis whose cause is the spiritual condition of the modern world. That condition is characterized by loss – the loss of religious certainties and of transcendence with its larger horizons...the miracles of technology have generally been more important. This is the cause of our spiritual crisis.

Another western voice, Hans Kung, exploring paths to constructive dialogue among world religions, notes that:

Religion always deals with an experiential "encounter with the Holy...whether this "sacred reality" be understood as power, as force (Spirits, demons, angels), as (a personal) God, as an (impersonal Divine, or an ultimate reality (nirvana). Hence "religion" can be paraphrased, for the purposes of our dialogue, as follows. Religion is a social and individual relationship, vitally realized in a tradition and community (through doctrine, ethos, and generally ritual as well) with something that transcends or encompasses man and his world...In contrast to philosophy, religion is concerned at once with a message of salvation and the way to salvation...Religion can be lived traditionally, superficially, passively, or in a profoundly sensitive, committed, dynamic way...Religion provides a comprehensive meaning for life, guarantees supreme values and unconditional norms, creates a spiritual community and home.

Heschel put the matter this way:

Religion is an answer to...ultimate questions, the moment we become oblivious to ultimate questions religion becomes irrelevant, and its crisis sets in. The primary task of philosophy of religion is to rediscover the questions to which religion is an answer. The inquiry must proceed both by delving into the consciousness...as well as by delving into the teachings and attitudes of the religious tradition.

As for a specific religion, and on a more personal level, In the book, *With Head and Heart: The Autobiography of Howard Thurman*, Dr. Thurman, while visiting Ceylon, answers a critic regarding his embracement of a faith (Christianity) categorically complicit in the oppression and dehumanization of peoples of African descent in the Americas. Dr. Thurman replied:

> I told him that I was not there to bolster a declining and disgraced Christian faith, nor did I come to make converts to Christianity. It is far from my purpose to symbolize anyone or anything. I think the religion of Jesus in its true genius offers me a promising way to work through the conflicts of a disordered world. I make careful distinction between Christianity and the religion of Jesus. My judgment about slavery and racial prejudice relative to Christianity is far more devastating than yours could ever be...the religion of Jesus

projected a creative solution to the pressing problem of survival for the minority of which he was a part in the Greco-Roman world. When Christianity became an imperial and world religion, it marched under banners other than that of the teacher and prophet of Galilee.

M. Shawn Copeland in The Modern Theologians: An Introduction to Christian Theology in the Twentieth Century (Edited by David F. Ford) surveys perspectives on religious experience (in terms of comparative theologies). She cites groups, experiences and perspectives that are intentionally marginalized in America and the West (Black, Hispanic/Latino, and Native American theologies) who are now coming out of the periphery of American religious life, into their own distinct and valid realities. She argues:

When confronted by the brutal history of misery to which the masses of human persons are subjected, theology would not go unmoved. It turns from philosophical hermeneutic to dialectics and ideology critique, to social (i.e.., political, economic, and technological), liberative, and emancipatory priorities. With this conversion, theology has assumed critical interrogative, and emancipative modes of discourse that take up a range of questions put forward by religiously, intellectually, and morally differentiated consciousness; that strive to overcome the alienations of modernity, i.e., secular from sacred, private from public, objectivity from subjectivity, thought from feelings, theory from practice; and that contest cooptation by structures of domination and resist the destructive experience of being dominated. This conversation constitutes a shift in paradigm; theology embraces a commitment to the historical as well as spiritual emancipation and liberation of oppressed, marginalized, and poor people in their particular cultural and social situations...Black, Hispanic/Latino, and Native American theologies are critical epistemic rejections of the equation of concepts with reality, of the reduction of knowledge to merely subjective or sense experience, of the attempt to ground knowledge in or on a prior first principles. These theologies expose not only the western idealization of reason, but the modern liberal romanticization of emotion as characteristic of Black, Hispanic/Latino, and Native American communities and cultures. Second, many scholars would concede that the worldview or mentality shaped and mediated by classical Greek philosophy and science has collapsed...Black, Hispanic/Latino, and Native American theologies come out of communities which have survived the brutish hegemony of white supremacist rule in America. Each of these theologies arises from communities which have been betrayed by a Christianity deeply implicated, not only in conquest and colonization of the Americas, but also in its invention. Each of these theologies can draw upon legacies of vigorous historical armed and negotiated resistance to cultural genocide, enslavement, exploitation, and marginalization.

Rebecca S. Chopp (pp 409-417) addresses this question from the perspective of Latin American Liberation Theology:

Latin American liberation theology speaks of God as manifest in the poor...for it arises out of the poor's experience of God. Like many other theologies, this one grows out of and reflects back upon faith itself...liberation theology seeks to speak of this faith and thus speak of God; in so doing it seeks to give voice to liberation, which involves not only freedom from oppression but also freedom to become new subjects of history.

Liberation theology and the faith upon which it reflects does not try to make the poor rich, or the rich poor, or some intermediary in between. Rather, the experience of and reflection of God and the poor seek to guide the transformation of all human beings into new ways of being human, ways not dependent upon structures of division between rich and poor, the common and the despised, the persons and nonpersons of history.

She speaks of Gustavo Gutierrez saying that:

> Gutierrez, perhaps the most influential of all Latin American liberation theologians, has made his theology the language of God from the perspective of the poor...Gustavo Gutierrez has been, for good reason, one of the primary interpreters of liberation theology. Gutierrez's work moves in a radically new interpretation of Christianity; Gutierrez has taken the basic symbols of Christian experience, and radically reworked them amid the experience of God's presence in the poor, but likewise, he has used the classical symbols of Christianity to give voice to the experience of the poor in history. In so doing, Gutierrez has

uncovered, for many of us, the presuppositions of power, dominance, and injustice in our basic theological beliefs.

Women's spiritual/religious experiences and perspectives (long minimized and suppressed by men and structures/system of male domination, have, to the progressing liberation and enrichment of many, come to fore. By way of personal exploration, historian Elaine Pagels, comments on the consequential differences, and distinctions between belief and actual experience in religion and related issues of tradition, organization, and institution:

> I had never thought much about an intimate relationship with God. It was more about how one lives in the universe and the power of religious tradition. Christianity was like the cultural language I spoke that was most familiar to me. Of course, it could have been Buddhist or anything else, but Christianity was what I had to contend with. My research deepened my relationship to Christianity, but it also alienated me from a lot of the institutional structures. That frustration and alienation emerged in my work, and it spoke to people who had shared those experiences – the desire for

an authentic spiritual connection and the disappointment in not finding social environments in which to share with other people and celebrate with them. Traditions have to be changed, and they always have been changed. We received it through millennia of transmission, revision, transformation, elimination, suppression, and addition. It's always been part of a living tradition, or it wouldn't have survived, and we change it every time we receive and live it...My work has nothing to do with participation in dogma and much to do with the care of the human community. It has to do with how the tradition became the way it did, what about it I can love, or not love at all.

Continuing to speak experientially (in relation to the early and separate deaths of her young son and husband), which indirectly relates to her book, *The Origin of Satan*, she goes on to say:

When I was dealing with so much pain and so much conflict in my life, the story of early Christianity, which involved so much pain and conflict, emerged. All this was suppressed in the Christian tradition and overlooked in scholarship, but I saw it because of what I was experiencing. What I was writing had little to do directly with the loss of people you deeply love, but the writing came with a sense that it was dealing with what I had to look at. So much scholarship about early Christianity is apologetic. The work that I do in these texts is highly imagistic. It appeals to quite a number of women because it speaks to layers of experience that women tune into very well, some men, too, of course. As women move into the place of spiritual leadership, they are making a difference in how religion is experienced – they shift hierarchy, balance, and expectation...The sensibility is different, as you know.

In *Beyond Belief* she brings fourth matters of belief and experience once again:

I am a historian of religion...I wondered when and how being a Christian became virtually synonymous with accepting a certain set of beliefs...I know from my own encounters with people...believers, agnostics and seekers- as well as people who don't belong to any church – that what matters in religious experience involves much more than what we believe (or what we do not believe). What is Christianity, and what is religion, I wondered, and why do so many of us still find it compelling, whether or not we belong to a church, and despite difficulties we may have with particular beliefs or practices?

Karen Armstrong, a respected and established authority of international acclaim on comparative religion, author of many books (her autobiographical, *The Spiral Staircase: My Climb Out of Darkness, Through the Narrow Gate, A History of God, The Battle for God* and numerous other works) and several documentaries on religious matters said in the *Spiral Staircase*:

> Writing Through the Narrow Gate has been an act of restoration and self-discovery. It had redeemed the time I had spent in the religious life and set it in proper perspective. As I had unearthed more and more layers of the experience, I had felt that I was reclaiming my past...When I had written the last pages...I realized that those years had probably been the most significant of my life; they had changed me forever. I might have lost my faith, I could no longer believe in God or the doctrines of the church, but I still longed for the sense of transcendence that the convent had promised to give me...It was true that I was no longer a Roman Catholic; it was true that

the convent experience had been damaging in many ways; and true that I had no intention of going back. It was true that I wasn't even a Christian any longer, and that the mere thought of going to church made me feel physically sick. Interviewers constantly congratulated me on my triumph over adversity, and for getting rid of an imbecilic religious worldview....Yet I was uneasily aware that this was not the whole truth. I was not that joyous girl, leaping in the air happy and at ease with the world, wholly integrated with secular life...that I no longer had any hunger for what I used to call God. By writing *Through The Narrow Gate* I had recalled and thus reawakened some of that longing for the sacred that had carried me into the religious life. But what could I realistically do with this nostalgia for transformation and transcendence? In a world that was now empty of God, I could see no place for it and did not understand what, if anything, it meant.

In an article published in the Christian Century magazine, Delores Williams (assistant professor of theology at Drew University Divinity School) speaks from another point of view to the necessity of "re-imaging" in spiritual life and theological reflection. The task of "re-imaging" is to reflect on and interpret spiritual life in "womanist" perspectives, in this instance, the experiences in faith of African American women. Speaking out of a Christian framework (as does Pagels and Armstrong) Williams argues that it is necessary to "shade in a context, to find a usable past so that we can construct a redemptive present."

She constructs a redemptive view of Jesus of Nazareth as a surrogate figure that black women can constructively identify with, viewing Jesus as "...the ultimate surrogate figure for our redemption." She asks, "In his life, then, was Jesus a divine mammy, nurturing other people's children, giving them the sustenance they needed to stand between themselves and the old, cold world? In this sense, her point of view is that Jesus became human to be made mammy."

Representative Tribal Voices (Native American)

Called "one of the great interpreters of religion in America," Vine Deloria Jr. of the Standing Rock Sioux makes several vital points from a Native perspective about religion, in his book, *God is Red: A Native view of Religion*:

Religion cannot be kept within the bounds of sermons and scripture. It is force in and of itself and it calls for the integration of lands and peoples in harmonious unity. The lands wait for those who can discern their rhythms. Who will listen to the tree, the animals and birds, the voices of the places of the land? As the long forgotten peoples of the respective continents rise and began to reclaim their ancient heritage, they will discover the meaning of the lands of their ancestors. That is when the invaders of the North American continent will discover that, for this land, God is red.

He speaks as one who had something of extreme value taken from him. Something is lost and must vigilantly be found and reclaimed. In this case, it's a relationship with the earth and all within it, he knows and feels. Something quite different from the "invaders."

Deloria also affirms the centrality of "relationship" in tribal religion: "The task of tribal religion, if such a relations can be said to have a task, is to determine that proper relationship that the people of the tribe must have with other living things."

George Tinker (Osage Nation) addresses the significance of relationship in tribal religion: the Lakota and Dakota peoples have a phrase used in all their prayers that aptly illustrates the Native American sense of the centrality of creation. The phrase, "Mitakuye Oyasin" (For all my relations) is polyvalent in its meaning...one is praying for one's close kin...And "relations" can be understood as tribal members or even all Indian people. At the same time, the phrase includes all human beings...proper relations with the Creator includes recognizing ourselves "as mere creatures" and "as part of, and integrally related to all creation."

V. F. Cordova, Ph.D. (Apache), writes that the world is defined by Euroman (the white people), as "hostile" and "wild...he is a creation of an extraterrestrial god, who has set man in an alien environment...In contrast, the universe of the Native American is based on the concept of harmony." This leads to the idea that man, a part of the universe, adapts himself to, and be responsible for, the continuing harmony he sees. In just a few words, she describes these two very different orientations to life and existence. It's clear which orientation is most conducive to life.

Representative Middle Eastern, Asian, And African Voices On Religion

African religions (from Western perspectives) have been woefully misunderstood, misinterpreted, generally maligned and regularly dismissed. One African scholar/theologian, John Mbiti, critically addresses and corrects this substandard and biased approach to the traditional religions of Africa.

In *African Religions and Philosophy,* Mbiti enlarges our knowledge of African traditional religions, noting that:

> Africans are notoriously religious, and each people has its own religious system with a set of beliefs and practices...We speak of African traditional religions in the plural because there are about one thousand African peoples (tribes), and each has its own religious system...To ignore these traditional beliefs, attitudes and practices can only lead to a lack of understanding African behavior and problems. Religion is the strongest element in traditional background, and exerts probably the greatest influence upon the thinking and living of the people

concerned...Because traditional religions permeate all the departments of life, there is no formal distinction between the sacred and the secular, between the religious and non-religious, between the spiritual and the material areas of life. Wherever the African is, there is his religion...Although many African languages do not have a word for religion as such, it nevertheless accompanies the individual from long before his birth to long after his physical death.

Moving from traditional African religions to the appearance of Christianity in Africa, Mbiti goes on to inform and remind us that:

Christianity in Africa is so old that it can rightly be described as an indigenous, traditional and African religion. Long before the start of Islam in the seventh century, Christianity was well established all over North Africa, Egypt, parts of Sudan and Ethiopia. It was a dynamic form of Christianity, producing great scholars and theologians like Tertullian, Origen, Clement of Alexandria and Augustine. African Christianity made a great contribution to Christendom through scholarship, participation in Church councils, defense of the Faith, movements like monasticism, theology, translation and preservation of the Scriptures, martyrdom, the famous Catechetical School of Alexandria, liturgy and even heresies and controversies.

The Circle of Concerned African Women

Theologians, established in Accra, Ghana (1989), by nearly 100 African women from within the continent, is an extremely vital entity/enterprise for creative research, writing, reading, fellowship, and dissemination of literature expressing and addressing the feelings, thoughts, interests, considerations, and concerns of African women.

Mercy Amba Oduyoye, in a paper entitled, **Gender and Theology in Africa Today,** sets forth the necessity for the tasks and endeavors African women are undertaking:

> In Africa gender became a theological issue when the Circle asserted that the gender parameter in African culture, and African religions have crucial effects on women's lives and on how womanhood is viewed by Africans...They examined daily relationships in marriage, inheritance laws and women's leadership and roles in wider society as in the church. Gender as the power, priority and preference of the

biological male over the biological female was evident everywhere. The women pointed out that it is not only biblical hermeneutics that needed attention, but most immediately, cultural hermeneutics as Africans are in crisis about their relationships to the inherent ways of doing and thinking...Gender in biblical studies took the form of re-reading, and the hermeneutic of suspicion and resistance prevailed.

Gwinyai H. Muzorewa writes of problems (since the modern introduction of Christianity to sub-Saharan Africa – 18th and 19th centuries) Africans had and continue to have (particularly with European/Western Christianity). He notes in his book, *The Origins and Development of African Theology*:

It was the spirit of African nationalism and Pan-Africanism that opened my eyes to the apparent contradictions between the Gospel of Jesus Christ as it was proclaimed in the mission churches and the African social reality as I experienced it. At times, it appeared as if the politicians spoke to my needs more than the preachers did. Because theology is one of the very few disciplines that attempts to deal with

African life holistically, I have developed tremendous and lifetime interests in it.

What does it have to say to, and about, the African who finds himself or herself in a situation where the very agency of the gospel of Jesus Christ turns out to be inseparable from the agency of oppression, racism, and dehumanization? How can the same agency preach meaningfully about love, humanity, liberation, and human dignity? This concern is what prompts my interest in theology.

Other African theologians, Idowu (1965), Mbiti (1980), Appiah-Kubi (1974) creatively address identical concerns in their efforts to express and address the realities of spiritual life, spirituality, and religion in Africa (past and present).

In his book, *Toward a True Kinship of Faith*: *How the World's Religions Can Come Together,* the Tibetan Buddhist spiritual leader, His Holiness, the Fourteenth Dalai Lama (Tenzin Gyatso) expresses his hope for the religions of the world:

Despite the tremendous progress in material conditions the world over, suffering remains. The afflictions such as greed, anger, hatred, and envy that underpinned much of our misery thousands of years ago continue to do so even today. Unless there is a radical change in human nature within a rapid period of time, these afflictions will plague us for many centuries to come. The teachings of each of the world's great religions, in their own unique way, have been and will continue to be a spiritual resource to counter the effects of these afflictions.

Therefore, religion remains relevant and will have an important role in human society for the foreseeable future. Supremely, the religions have inspired the flow of compassion and great acts of altruism, the effects of which have resonated in the lives of millions. So, both from the point of view of peace in the world, and to foster the beneficial potential of religion in the world, the faith traditions must find a way of relating to each other with mutual acceptance and genuine respect.

He sees compassion as the universal key to religion:

One of the special joys I have come to appreciate in my journey down the spiritual paths of other faiths is the wonderful privilege of opening my heart and hearing the voice of other traditions speaking clearly and directly. This place of sharing, rooted in the heart, is connected to the fact that the great religions themselves urge their practitioners to open their hearts and let compassion blossom as the core message for living an ethical life...The great religions have the power to lift our hearts and raise our minds to an elevated expanse of joy and understanding through their shared teachings on compassion.

Relational Qualities: Rooted in Love

All of these relational qualities specific to **Relational Spirituality** are rooted in love. Love however, does not mean the same thing to all people. Some individuals equate love with the thrills of romance and the unarguable power of sex. Others see love as doing one's duty, meeting obligations, and providing or being provided for by others. For yet others, love involves the sharing of vital spiritual life, grand dreams, compelling visions, inspirational hopes, challenging endeavors and significant life purposes.

Most languages have a word or words for love. Generally speaking, English has one, with various shades of meaning. Spanish and Greek each have at least three words for love. Indian Sanskrit has as many as ninety-six words for love. The Persian language contains eighty words for love. Love is a cardinal theme in spiritual life, spirituality and religion too:

- Christians may call it agape (an active compassionate unselfish love).

  - Jews may call it ahavah expressing (the utmost depth in personal and divine relationships).

  - Hindus may call it prema (a deep spiritual love of God who is love itself).

  - Buddhists may call it metta (an active love expressing good will towards all).

  - Muslims may recite a statement from the Prophet Muhammed "Do you love your Creator? Love your fellow beings first."

  - Followers of Confucius may call it ren (the essence of love shared among human beings).

Whatever comparative differences, similarities, or disagreements there may be in the arena of global spirituality, there is universal recognition of the centrality and necessity of love in our lives. We instinctively know that love enlivens, uplifts, comforts and heals us. Without love in our lives we become depressed and distraught.

Deepak Chopra, in his book *The Path of Love: Spiritual Strategies for Healing*, lists a number of vital experiences that love brings about:

> Love is meant to heal.
> Love is meant to renew.
> Love is meant to make us safe.
> Love is meant to inspire with its power.
> Love is meant to make us certain without doubt.
> Love is meant to oust all fear.
> Love is meant to unveil immortality.
> Love is meant to bring peace.
> Love is meant to harmonize differences.
> Love is meant to bring us closer to God.

The noted psychologist Viktor E. Frankl (1905-1997), author of *Man's Search for Meaning,* a holocaust survivor and creator of Logotherapy, left us with these words about authentic love:

Love is the only way to grasp another human being in the innermost core of his personality. No one can become fully aware of the very essence of another human being unless he loves him. By the spiritual act of love, he is enabled to see the essential traits and features in the beloved person, and even more, he sees that, which is potential in him, that which is not yet actualized but yet ought to be actualized. Furthermore, by his love, the loving person enables the beloved person to actualize these potentialities by making him aware of what he can be and what he should become. He makes these potentialities come true.

The apostle Saul, (aka) Paul, summed up the meaning of authentic love this way:

If I speak in the tongues of men or of angels, but do not have love, I am only a resounding gong or a clanging cymbal. [2] If I have the gift of prophecy and can fathom all mysteries and all knowledge, and if I have a faith that can move mountains, but do not have love, I am nothing. [3] If I give all I possess to the poor and give over my body to hardship that I may boast, but do not have love, I gain nothing.
[4] Love is patient, love is kind. It does not envy, it does not boast, it is not proud. [5] It does not dishonor others, it is not self-

seeking, it is not easily angered, it keeps no record of wrongs. ⁶ Love does not delight in evil but rejoices with the truth. ⁷ It always protects, always trusts, always hopes, always perseveres.

⁸ Love never fails. But where there are prophecies, they will cease; where there are tongues, they will be stilled; where there is knowledge, it will pass away. ⁹ For we know in part and we prophesy in part, ¹⁰ but when completeness comes, what is in part disappears. ¹¹ When I was a child, I talked like a child, I thought like a child, I reasoned like a child. When I became a man, I put the ways of childhood behind me. ¹² For now we see only a reflection as in a mirror; then we shall see face to face. Now I know in part; then I shall know fully, even as I am fully known. And now these three remain: faith, hope and love. But the greatest of these is love (1ˢᵗ Corinthians, Ch.13).

These **relational qualities** and the corresponding conduct associated with them must not be blown out of proportion. It would not be wise to overstate them as if they were the only relational qualities needful, necessary or available for individuals and groups to embrace and nurture. They are not put forward to merely gain attention or create unrealizable expectations that are impossible to fulfill. The relational qualities of R/S ought, can and must be *realized within relationship*, as they (alongside other positive, equally requisite qualities) are what deepen, enrich and enhance our lives and keep the light of life ablaze among us. As stated earlier, R/S is costly and exacting. There is nothing easy about it. It takes all we have, and then some. It involves who we are, and who we are becoming. Much more than either reform or revolution, it requires radical change within oneself.

CHAPTER TEN
Relational Spirituality (R/S): A Reflective Summation

If the GSC, representative of all faiths, paths, and traditions), actively embraced R/S, nothing short of a spiritual transformation would occur that would affect every conceivable relationship and every dimension of life.

If key representatives of every religion and/or spiritual paths were committed to group/individual *transformation,* together, they could *transcend,* what, up to this present now, are   blocks, and impediments of *self-seeking, self-serving, self-interest*. If the GSC would do so, greater spiritual light would blaze brightly benefitting all people in every quarter of the globe.

In collegial terms, if those in *spiritual leadership* as ministers, teachers, doctors, practitioners, pastors, priests, rabbis, imams, mullahs, shamans, guides and mentors would move from mere talk/assent of R/S, to its actualization in the issues of everyday life, people everywhere would become convinced of its authenticity and enthusiastically embrace their collective examples.

If R/S is authentically embraced, the usual socio-cultural-political-class-ethnic-racial-tribal-gender-sexual antipathies and divisions would begin to heal, and lives once broken, shattered, and crushed would become whole, hopeful, promising and healthy.

If my colleagues engaged in various other spiritual ministries would construct their endeavors around *the centrality of relationships*, in contrast to the usual prioritizations of doctrine, customs, and tradition, conflict, division, discord, and strife would be replaced with harmony, peace, and unity, the essential ingredients for a purposeful, productive, and creative life. Of course, none of this will be easy. R/S is exacting and will take our measure. Many, consequently, will "try" Relational Spirituality only to soon abandon it before its fruit can become evident, others (individuals and groups) will, undeterred, stay the course and see triumph upon triumph. My plea is that the Global Spiritual Community will shoulder-up to, recover and actively reclaim that relational center it still as yet, needs to find anew. It's late in the day, but still time to actualize the axiom:

While many things matter in spiritual life, spirituality and religion, our actual relationships (their quality or lack thereof) matter most – more than any other competing, interest, consideration, and concern. Come, all. Let us find God, together.

R.E.A (Oluwafemi)

BIBLIOGRAPHY

American Heritage Dictionary (2000). Online

Armstrong, Karen (2004). *The Spiral Staircase.* NY: Anchor Books Random House Inc.

Bertine, Eleanor (1992). *Close Relationships: Family, Friendship, Marriage.* Toronto: Inner City Books

Buber, Martin (1958). *I and Thou.* NY: Charles Scribner's Sons.

Britannica Concise Encyclopedia (2006). Online

Butterworth, Eric (1969). *Unity of All Life.* NY: Harper and Row Publishers.

Chopra, Deepak (1997). *The Path to Love: Spiritual Strategies for Healing.* NY: Three Rivers Press.

Cruse, Harold (1967). *The Crisis of the Negro Intellectual.* Y: William Morrow & Company.

Deloria, Vine (1994). *God is Red: A Native View of Religion.* NY: The Putnam Publishing Group.

―――― (1999). *For this Land: Writings on Religion in America.* NY, London: Routledge.

Dillaway, Newton (Ed.), (1939). *The Gospel of Emerson.* MA: The Montrose Press

Drucker, Malka (2002). *White Fire: A Portrait of Women Spiritual Leaders in America.* VA: SkyLight Paths Publishing.

Dubois, W.E.B. (1968). *The Autobiography of W.E.B. Dubois: A Soliloquy on Viewing My Life from the Last Decade of its First Century.* NY: International Publishers.

Fellows, Ward J. (1979). *Religions East and West.* NY: Holt, Rinehart and Winston.

Fillmore, Lowell (1964). *The Prayer Way to Health, Wealth, and Happiness.* MO: Unity School of Christianity.

Ford, David F. (Ed.), (1997). *The Modern Theologians: An Introduction to Christian Theology in the Twentieth Century.* MA: Blackwell Publishers Ltd.

Fox, Emmett (1950). *Around the Year with Emmett Fox.* CA: HarperCollins.

Frankl, Viktor (1959). *Man's Search for Meaning.* NY: Beacon Press.

Glazer, Nathan (1965). *Ethnic Dilemmas: 1964-1982.* MA: Harvard University Press.

Goldsmith, Joel S. (1963). *A Parenthesis in Eternity.* Harper and Row, New York.

Gyatso, Tenzin (the Fourteenth Dalai Lama)(, (2010). *Toward a True Kinship of Faiths: How the World's Religions Can Come Together.* NY: Random House, Inc.

Hall, Calvin S. and Norby, Vernon J. (1973). *A Primer of Jungian Psychology.* NY: Penguin Books.

Heschel, Abraham (1955). *God in Search of Man: A Philosophy of Judaism*. NY: Farrar, Straus and Giroux, New York.

—— (1951). *Man is not Alone*: A Philosophy of Religion. NY: H. Wolff.

James, William (1958). *The Varieties of Religious Experience: A Study in Human Nature.* NY: The New American Library of World Literature, Inc.

Jung, C.G. (1938). *Psychology and Religion.* CT: Yale University Press, Inc.

—— (1964). Collected Works Vol. 10:397.

King Jr., Martin Luther (1991). *A Testament of Hope: The Essential Writings of Martin Luther King Jr.* HarperCollins Publishers, New York, NY.

Kung, Hans (2004). *Christianity: Essence, History, and Future.* NY: The Continuum International Publishing Group Inc.

Malefijt, Annemarie de Waal (1968) *Religion and Culture.* NY: Macmillan.

McGreal, Ian P. (Ed.), (1995). *Great Thinkers of the Eastern World.* NY: HarperCollins, Inc.

Masters, Paul Leon (1978). Ministers Course Study Lesson V.1, (Lessons 1-4). CA: Studio City.

—— (2011).

Mbiti, John S. (1970). *African Religions and Philosophy*. NY: Anchor Books/Doubleday & Company, Inc.

Merriam- Webster's Collegiate Dictionary (2006). Online

Muzorewa, Gwinyai H. (1985). *The Origins and Development of African Theology*. NY: Orbis Books.

Niebuhr, Reinhold (1955). *Moral Man and Immoral Society*. Charles Scribner's Sons

Oduyeyo, Mercy Amba (2001) The proceedings of the Convocation of African Women Theologians. Ibadan. Nigeria: Daystar Press

O'Neal David (1996). *Meister Eckhart, from Whom God Hid Nothing, Sermons, Writings and Sayings: New Seeds, Boston and London*

Pagels, Elaine (2003). *Beyond Belief*. NY: Random House, Inc.

Penguin Dictionary of Religion (1997). Online

Smith, Curtis D. (1990). *Jung's Quest for Wholeness*. NY: State University of New York Press.

Smith, Houston (1958). *The World's Religions*. NY: HarperCollins Publishers, p.183.

—— (2001). *Why Religion Matters: The Fate of the Human Spirit in an Age of Disbelief.* NY: HarperCollins.

Storr, Anthony (1988). *Solitude: A Return to the Self.* NY: The Free Press.

Thurman, Howard (1979). *With Head and Heart: The Autobiography of Howard Thurman.* NY: Harcourt, Brace, Jovanovich.

Tinker, George (1991). *For all My Relations: Justice, Peace and Integrity Of Christmas Trees.* Sojourners Magazine

Tolstoy, Leo (1894). *The Kingdom of God is Within You.* NY: Cassell Pub. Co., (1984). NE: University of Nebraska Press.

Troyat, Henri (1967). *Tolstoy.* NY: Doubleday & Company, Inc.

Wolman, Richard N. (2001). *Thinking with Your Soul.* NY: Harmony Books, New York, NY.

Index

A

Actual Relationships, 37, 42-43, 64, 67, 83, 92, 94-95, 177

African Nationalism, 166

African Religions, 163-165

African Religions and Philosophy, book, 163

African Theologians, 167

American Liberation Theology, 153

Analects of Confucius, 37

Anti-Religious Philosophy, 22

Armstrong, Karen, 159, 160

Authentic Spiritual Life, 63

B

Beloved Community, 113-116

Bertine, Eleanor, 41

Biblical Hermeneutics, 166

Big Religious Picture, 19

Brahman, 32-33, 110

Britannica Concise Encyclopedia, 146

Buber, Martin, 66

Buddha's Motivation, 37

Buddhism, 36

C

Centrality of Relationship, 16, 29, 33, 38, 50, 79, 90, 176

Centrality of the Intellect, 65

Chopra, Deepak, 171

Christ As Relational, 83

Christ's Invitational, 34

Christ's Relational Concern, 83

Christian Affliction, 81

Christianity in Africa, 164

Concerned African Women, 165

Confucianism, 35, 134

Constellation of Relationships, 31, 53, 91

Conventional Spirituality, 56, 59-60

Cultural Hermeneutics, 166

D

Delphic Council, 107

Divine Presence, 108-113, 121, 123-128, 130-133

E

Ecclesiastical Spirituality, 68-70

Empathetic Compassion, 36

Emphatic Concern, 38

Euroman, 162

F

Founders of Religion, 29, 31, 38, 40

Frankl, Viktor E., 171

G

Gautama, Siddhartha, 36

Glazer, Nathan, 70-71, 141-142

Global Entity, 27

Global Relational Mission, 32

Global Spiritual Enterprise (GSE), 19, 31

Group Spirituality, 70, 72-73, 78, 141

Guru's Instruction, 37

Gutierrez, Gustavo, 154

H

H., Muzorewa, Gwinyai, 166

Hallmark of Buddhism, 36

Heschel's Counsel, 17

Heschel, Rabbi Abraham, 17, 22, 102-103, 145, 149

Hinduism, 32-33, 110, 134

I

Incomprehensible Disconnect, 44

Indispensable Relational Qualities, 117

Inspirational Tract, 93

Institutionalized System, 146

Intellectual Priority, 60

Intellectual Spirituality, 60, 65, 67

Intellectual Theological Enterprise, 63

Inter-Religious Conflicts, 76

International Metaphysical Ministry (IMM), 110, 122

Intimacies of Relationship, 31-33

Islamic Faith, 35, 110, 134, 164

J

Judaism, 33, 35, 96, 105, 129, 144

Jung, C.G., 21, 42, 59, 65-66, 98-99, 106, 115

K

King, Martin Luther, 57-58, 114, 119, 132

M

Malefijt, Annemarie de Waal, 20

Man's Search for Meaning, book, 171

Merriam-Webster's Collegiate Dictionary, 145

Moral-Ethical Perfection, 95

Moral-Spiritual Imperatives, 44

Motivational Piece, 93

N

Nanak, Guru, 37

Native American, 152-154, 161-163

Niebuhr, Reinhold, 72

Nomenclatures, 80

O

Oduyoye, Mercy Amba, 165

Original Spiritual Concern (OSC), 29-30

P

Physical Wounds, 49

Political Problems, 23

Process of Prioritization, 55

Program for Religious Activism, 93

Pseudo-Spiritual Priorities, 56

Psycho-Spiritual, 42, 49, 51, 53, 65, 104, 118, 124, 131, 137

Psycho-Spiritual Tools, 108

Psychotherapeutic Systems, 21

R

Rationalistic Approach, 64

Realm of Relationship, 35, 38, 91, 116

Reciprocal Relationship, 33

Redemptive Concern, 88

Relational Center, 29-31, 40, 79, 176

Relational Emphases, 38

Relational Experiences, 47

Relational Obliviousness, 44

Relational Plight, 42

Relational Priority, 32, 43, 79, 91

Relational Problems, 94

Relational Qualities, 86, 117-118, 120, 123, 133, 171, 173-174

    Acceptance, 120-121

    Affirmation, 121-123

    Empathy, 125-126

    Encouragement, 124-125

    Justice, 131-132

    Peace, 128-129

    Power, 129-130

    Service, 126-127

Support, 123-124

Truth, 130-131

Unity, 127-128

Relational Spirituality (R/S), 64, 90-96, 99, 101, 108, 112-113, 115, 117, 120,123, 129-131, 133-136, 169, 174-176

Transcendence, 134-136, 138

Transformation, 134-136, 138

Transition, 134-136, 138

Triumph, 134-136, 138

Relationally Unconscious, 45

Religious Completion, 68

Religious Development, 82

Religious Polemics, 87

Religious Problem, 22

Religious System, 68, 95, 163

Representative Middle Eastern, 163

Russell, Bertrand, 45

Russian Orthodox Church, 68-69, 77

S

Sarai, 33

Service-Consciousness, 126

Shruti, 32

Sikh Faith, 37

Smith, Curtis D., 98

Smith, Houston, 147

Smith, Robert M., 118

Socio-Political Systems, 84

Spiral Staircase, book, 158

Spiritual Experience, 18-21, 27, 29-30, 32-33, 38, 41, 45-46, 53, 55, 59, 61, 64, 66, 73-74, 77-78, 84, 88, 127, 142, 146

Spiritual Finality, 68

Spiritual Leadership, 21, 52, 156, 174

Spiritual Life, 18-21, 25-26, 29-31, 40, 45, 47, 52-54, 59-60, 62-64, 68, 71, 83-84, 89-90, 93, 95, 111, 122, 137, 142, 159, 167, 169-170, 177

Spiritual Optics Test (SOT), 97-98

Storr, Anthony, 45

Supreme Ground of Being, 32

T

The Origin of Satan, book, 156

The Origins and Development of African, book, 166

The Path of Love, book, 171

Theologians, 151, 154, 164, 165

Theology, 33, 43, 62-63, 77, 82, 147, 152-155, 159, 164-167

Three Separate Entities, 100

Thurman, Howard, 150

Tinker, George, 162

Toward a True Kinship of Faith, book, 167

Traditional African Religions, 164

Traditional Theological Questions, 64

Traditional Theologies, 62

Transcendent Spiritual Source, 31, 51, 63, 91

U

Universal Phenomenon, 17, 36, 70

Upanishads, 32, 110

V

Vedic Age, 32

W

Williams, Delores, 159 -160

Made in the USA
Lexington, KY
02 April 2017